My First Story Book About Islam

Understanding Faith and Islamic Values from Stories

Aasma S.

My First Picture Book Inc.

Copyright © 2024 by My First Picture Book Inc.

All rights reserved.

No portion of this book may be reproduced in any form without written permission from the publisher or author, except as permitted by U.S. copyright law.

Contents

Introduction	1
1. The Beautiful Meaning of "Islam"	4
2. The Special Book Called the Quran	8
3. The Five Pillars of Islam	12
4. Understanding Shahada: The Declaration of Faith	16
5. Learning Salah: The Daily Prayers	20
6. The Importance of Zakat: Helping Those in Need	24
7. Sawm: Fasting During Ramadan	28
8. The Journey of Hajj: Pilgrimage to Mecca	32
9. Eid al-Fitr: The Festival of Breaking the Fast	36
10. Eid al-Adha: The Festival of Sacrifice	40
11. The Significance of the Mosque: A Place of Worship	44

12.	Learning Wudu: The Ablution Before Prayer	48
13.	The Call to Prayer: Adhan	52
14.	The Beauty of Islamic Art and Calligraphy	56
15.	Understanding Halal and Haram	60
16.	The Quranic Stories: Lessons for Life	64
17.	The Significance of the Hijab	68
18.	Jannah: The Gardens of Paradise	72
19.	Family Love in Islam	76
20.	The Role of the Imam: A Leader in the Community	80
21.	Sami's Path to Taqwa	84
22.	Sami Learns Patience: Sabr	88
23.	Adab: The Magic of Good Manners	92
24.	The Story of the Kaaba: The Sacred House	96
25.	Understanding Jumu'ah: The Friday Prayer	100
26.	The Story of Islamic Months: The Hijri Calendar	106
27.	The Night of Power: Laylat al-Qadr	110

28.	The Meaning of Bismillah: In the Name of Allah	114
29.	The Big Family of the Ummah	118
30.	Learning About Islamic Celebrations	122
31.	Understanding the Sunnah: Following the Prophet's Way	126
32.	The Role of the Mufti: Islamic Scholar	130
33.	The Story of the Mihrab: The Prayer Niche	134
34.	Understanding Dhikr: Remembrance of Allah	138
35.	The Story of Iman: Faith in Islam	142
36.	The Importance of Cleanliness in Islam	146
37.	The Story of Islamic Greetings: Salam	150
38.	Understanding Qibla: The Direction of Prayer	156
39.	The Role of Angels in Islam	160
40.	The Concept of Shura: Consultation	164
41.	The Importance of Knowledge in Islam	168
42.	The Story of the Islamic Dress Code	172

43.	Understanding Qadr: Divine Destiny	176
44.	The Story of Halaal Food	180
45.	The Importance of Fasting Beyond Ramadan	184
46.	The Concept of Amanah: Trustworthiness	188
47.	Understanding Qiyam: Standing in Prayer	192
48.	The Story of the Quranic Recitation: Tajweed	196
49.	The Role of the Quranic Schools: Madrasah	200
50.	Understanding the Concept of Barakah: Blessings	204

Introduction

Welcome to "My First Book About Islam"

Assalamu Alaikum! Welcome to "My First Book About Islam," a special book crafted just for you! This book is your doorway to the beautiful world of Islam, filled with engaging stories and simple explanations to help you learn about this amazing faith. We've designed each chapter with love and care, using easy-to-understand language to make learning about Islam fun and meaningful for young readers like you.

In this book, you'll embark on a journey through the wonderful teachings of Islam. You'll discover the meaning behind the word "Islam," the significance of the Quran, and the importance of saying "Bismillah" in our everyday lives. You'll learn about the Five Pillars of Islam, the stories behind Islamic greetings, and so much more.

With every page, you'll find yourself meeting inspiring characters, exploring new ideas, and understanding the beauty of living with kindness, honesty, and gratitude. You'll learn about the wonders of nature, the value of helping others, and the blessings that come with following the teachings of Allah.

Our goal is to help you grow closer to Allah, appreciate His guidance, and find joy in the lessons of Islam. We hope these stories inspire you to be compassionate, thoughtful, and full of faith every day.

So, open your heart and mind, and get ready to explore the incredible teachings in "My First Book About Islam." May your journey be filled with love, wisdom, and blessings!

Happy reading, and may Allah's peace and mercy be with you always!

Chapter 1

The Beautiful Meaning of "Islam"

In a small village, there lived a boy named Ahmed. Ahmed was a curious and kind-hearted boy who loved to ask questions about everything he saw. He loved learning about the world around him.

One sunny day, Ahmed's parents took him to the mosque. The mosque was a beautiful building with tall minarets and a big dome. It was a place where people came to pray and learn about Allah. Ahmed was very excited to visit the mosque.

When they arrived, Ahmed saw many people smiling and greeting each other with "As-salamu alaykum." Everyone seemed happy and peaceful. Ahmed's Baba took his hand and led him inside. They found a quiet corner, and Baba began to explain something very special to him.

"Ahmed," Baba said, "do you know what the word 'Islam' means?"

Ahmed shook his head. "No, Baba. What does it mean?"

His Baba smiled and said, "Islam means 'peace' and 'submission.'"

Ahmed's eyes widened. "What does 'submission' mean, Baba?"

His Baba explained, "Submission means to listen and follow. In Islam, we listen to and follow Allah's teachings. This helps us live in peace with ourselves, with others, and with the world."

Ahmed thought about this for a moment. "How do we submit to Allah, Baba?"

His Baba answered, "We submit to Allah by praying, being kind to others, helping those in need, and following the teachings of the Quran."

Ahmed remembered how his parents always prayed five times a day. He also remembered how they helped their neighbors and shared their food with the poor. Now he understood why they did these things.

As they walked home from the mosque, Ahmed saw a girl named Aisha playing with her little brother. She smiled and waved at Ahmed. Ahmed smiled back and felt a warm feeling in his heart. He thought about how happy everyone seemed when they were kind and helpful.

The next day, Ahmed decided to try to submit to Allah in his own way. He woke up early to pray with his parents. He helped his Ummi with the dishes and shared his toys with his little sister. When he saw an old man struggling to carry his bags, Ahmed ran over and helped him.

"Shukran, young man," the old man said, smiling.

Ahmed felt very happy. He realized that submitting to Allah and being kind made him feel peaceful and joyful. He liked this feeling and wanted to keep doing good things every day.

One evening, Ahmed's Ummi told him a story about Prophet Muhammad (peace be upon him). She said, "The Prophet Muhammad always taught us to be kind and helpful. He showed us how to live in peace and harmony with everyone."

Ahmed listened carefully and felt proud to follow the teachings of the Prophet Muhammad. He wanted to be just like him.

From that day on, Ahmed tried his best to be a good Muslim. He prayed, helped others, and was kind to everyone he met. He learned that by submitting to Allah, he could live a life full of peace.

Moral of the Story: Being kind and helpful to others makes us feel peaceful and happy.

Chapter 2

The Special Book Called the Quran

In a lovely village, there lived a boy named Hassan. Hassan was a cheerful and curious boy who loved listening to stories. One evening, Hassan's Ummi sat down with him and said, "Today, I will tell you about a very special book called the Quran."

Hassan's eyes lit up. "What is the Quran, Ummi?" he asked excitedly.

His Ummi smiled and said, "The Quran is the holy book of Islam. It was given to us by Allah. The Quran teaches us how to live a good life and be kind to others."

Hassan listened carefully. "How did we get the Quran, Ummi?"

His Ummi explained, "Many years ago, Allah sent a special angel named Jibril to a man named Prophet Muhammad (peace be upon him). The angel Jibril told Prophet Muhammad the words of Allah. Prophet Muhammad then shared these words with everyone, and they were written down to make the Quran."

Hassan was amazed. "So, the Quran is from Allah?"

"Yes," his Ummi said. "The Quran is Allah's message to us. It tells us how to pray, be honest, and help others. It also teaches us about Allah and how much He loves us."

Hassan's Ummi then took out a beautiful book with a shiny cover. "This is our Quran," she said. She opened it and showed Hassan the Arabic words inside. "These words are very special and important."

Hassan touched the pages gently. "What do the words say, Ummi?"

His Ummi replied, "The Quran tells us many things. It teaches us to be kind to our family and friends. It tells us to share with those who don't have enough. It reminds us to pray to Allah every day."

Hassan thought about his friends and how he could be kind to them. "Can I learn to read the Quran, Ummi?" he asked eagerly.

"Of course, Hassan," his Ummi said. "We will start learning together. Many Muslims around the world read the Quran every day. It helps us feel close to Allah and understand how to be good people."

Hassan felt happy. He wanted to be close to Allah and be a good person too. He sat down with his Ummi, and they began to read the Quran together. His Ummi helped him say the words slowly and carefully.

As they read, Hassan felt peaceful and loved. He liked learning about the kind and wise teachings of Allah. His Ummi told him stories from the Quran about how Prophet Muhammad (peace be upon him) was always kind and helpful to others. Hassan wanted to be just like him.

Every day, Hassan and his Ummi read a little more of the Quran. He learned how to pray, be honest, and help others. He felt proud to follow the teachings of the Quran. He liked sharing with his friends and helping his neighbors, just like the Quran taught him.

One day, Hassan's Abba joined them. "The Quran is not just a book to read," he said. "It's a guide for how we live our lives. It helps us make good choices and be happy."

Hassan nodded. He understood now how special the Quran was. It was more than just words on a page. It was a way to live a good, kind, and happy life.

Moral of the Story: Reading the Quran teaches us to be kind, helpful, and close to Allah.

Chapter 3

The Five Pillars of Islam

In a peaceful village, there lived a boy named Yasin. Yasin was a curious and cheerful boy who loved learning about his faith. One evening, as Yasin sat with his Ummi and Abu, they decided to teach him about the Five Pillars of Islam.

Ummi began, "The first pillar is Shahada. It means having faith. We say, 'La ilaha illallah, Muhammadur rasulullah.' This means, 'There is no god but Allah, and Muhammad is His messenger.'" Yasin's eyes sparkled as he repeated the words after his Ummi.

Abu then said, "The second pillar is Salah, which means prayer. We pray five times a day to talk to Allah and feel close to Him." He showed Yasin how to wash before praying. Together, they stood, bowed, and prostrated in prayer. Yasin felt a special connection with Allah when he prayed.

The next day, Ummi explained, "The third pillar is Zakat, which means giving to the poor. We share what we have with those who need help." Yasin remembered how they always gave food and clothes to their neighbors who didn't have enough. He felt happy knowing they were helping others. Ummi said, "When we give Zakat, we are helping to make the world a better place and showing kindness to those in need."

During the month of Ramadan, Yasin learned about the fourth pillar, Sawm, which means fasting. Ummi said, "We fast from sunrise to sunset to remember how blessed we are and to feel what it's like for those who have little to eat." Yasin tried to fast with his family. Although it was hard, he felt proud to be part of it. Ummi and Abu explained how fasting helps cleanse the body and mind, and how it brings them closer to Allah.

One evening, as they broke their fast with dates and water, Yasin's Abu told him about the fifth pillar, Hajj. "Hajj is a special journey to Mecca that Muslims try to make at least once in their lifetime. It helps us feel united with Muslims all around the world."

Yasin imagined the big, beautiful Kaaba in Mecca. He hoped to go there one day with his family. Abu told Yasin how millions of Muslims gather in Mecca, all dressed in simple white clothes, performing the same rituals. "It's a reminder that we are all equal in the eyes of Allah," Abu said.

One day, Yasin's grandfather, Jaddi, visited them. Jaddi had been to Hajj, and he shared his experiences with Yasin. "When I went to Mecca, I saw millions of Muslims all praying together. It was a beautiful sight. We wore simple white clothes and prayed around the Kaaba. It made me feel very close to Allah." Yasin listened intently, imagining the grandeur and spirituality of the pilgrimage.

Yasin loved hearing his Jaddi's stories. He felt proud of his faith and the Five Pillars that helped him be a good Muslim. He understood that these pillars were like strong supports that helped him live a good and meaningful life.

Every day, Yasin tried to remember the lessons from the Five Pillars. He repeated the Shahada with faith, prayed Salah with his family, gave Zakat to those in need, fasted during Ramadan, and dreamed of going to Hajj one day. He felt proud when he helped his friends and neighbors, knowing he was following the teachings of Islam.

Ummi and Abu were very proud of Yasin. They knew he was learning to live a good life by following the Five Pillars of Islam. Yasin felt happy and peaceful, knowing he was growing closer to Allah. He loved being part of a community that shared such beautiful and meaningful traditions.

Moral of the Story: Following the Five Pillars of Islam helps us be good, kind, and close to Allah.

Chapter 4

Understanding Shahada: The Declaration of Faith

Ali was playing in the garden when he heard his Jadda calling him from the house. He ran inside, curious about what she wanted to share with him. Jadda had a gentle smile on her face and a twinkle in her eye as she patted the seat next to her.

"Ali, I want to tell you about something very special today," she began. "It's called the Shahada."

Ali sat down, eager to listen. "What is the Shahada, Jadda?" he asked, his eyes wide with curiosity.

Jadda smiled warmly and said, "The Shahada is the declaration of faith in Islam. It's the first and most important pillar of Islam. The words are: 'La ilaha illallah, Muhammadur rasulullah,' which means, 'There is no god but Allah, and Muhammad is His messenger.'"

Ali repeated the words slowly after Jadda, trying to pronounce them correctly. "La ilaha illallah, Muhammadur rasulullah."

"Very good, Ali!" said Jadda. "These words are very special. They show our belief in the oneness of Allah and that Prophet Muhammad (peace be upon him) is His messenger."

Ali thought about this for a moment. "Jadda, why is the Shahada so important?"

Jadda explained, "The Shahada is important because it's the foundation of our faith. When we say the Shahada, we are showing our commitment to Allah. It's the first step in being a Muslim. Saying the Shahada with belief in our hearts means we accept Islam and all its teachings."

Just then, Ali's older brother, Akhi Bilal, walked in. He had just come from the mosque. "As-salamu alaykum! I see you're learning about the Shahada, Ali," Bilal said with a smile. "Do you know that we say the Shahada in our prayers every day? It reminds us of our faith and keeps us connected to Allah."

Ali nodded, feeling proud. "I want to remember it well and say it every day too."

Bilal suggested, "Let's make a special poster with the words of the Shahada and put it in your room. That way, you can see it every day and remember how important it is."

Excited, Ali and Bilal gathered some colorful markers and a big piece of paper. They carefully wrote the words "La ilaha illallah, Muhammadur rasulullah" in beautiful letters. Ali added some stars and hearts around the words to make it look special.

When they finished, they hung the poster on the wall in Ali's room. Ali looked at it with pride. "Alhamdulillah! Now I'll never forget the Shahada!" he said.

Later that evening, Ali's Baba came home from work. He saw the poster and smiled. "This is beautiful, Ali," he said. "The Shahada is not just words; it's a promise to live our lives according to Allah's guidance and to follow the teachings of Prophet Muhammad (peace be upon him)."

Ali felt a warm feeling in his heart. He understood that the Shahada was more than just words. It was a declaration of his faith and a promise to live a good and honest life.

Moral of the Story: The Shahada is the foundation of our faith, reminding us of our belief in Allah and His messenger.

Chapter 5

Learning Salah: The Daily Prayers

Amina loved spending time with her family and learning new things about her faith. One morning, as the sun began to rise, Amina's Ummi gently woke her up. "Amina, it's time to learn about Salah, the daily prayers," she said with a warm smile.

Amina rubbed her eyes and sat up, curious. "What is Salah, Ummi?" she asked.

Ummi began to explain, "Salah is the way we pray to Allah. Muslims pray five times a day. It helps us remember Allah and be thankful for everything He has given us."

Amina's eyes widened. "Five times a day? That sounds like a lot!" she said.

Ummi nodded. "Yes, Amina. But each prayer is special and has its own time of day. Let me teach you the names of the five prayers."

Ummi then recited, "Fajr is the morning prayer. Dhuhr is the midday prayer. Asr is the afternoon prayer. Maghrib is the evening prayer, and Isha is the night prayer."

Amina repeated the names after her Ummi, trying to remember them. "Fajr, Dhuhr, Asr, Maghrib, and Isha," she said slowly.

"Very good, Amina!" Ummi said. "Now, let's start with Fajr, the morning prayer. First, we need to do wudu, which is washing before we pray."

Amina followed her Ummi to the sink, where they washed their hands, mouth, nose, face, arms, head, and feet. "This feels nice and refreshing," Amina said, smiling.

After wudu, they laid out their prayer mats. Ummi showed Amina how to stand, bow, and prostrate during the prayer. They stood side by side and prayed Fajr together. Amina felt a warm and peaceful feeling as she prayed.

Later that day, when the sun was high in the sky, it was time for Dhuhr. Ummi reminded Amina, "It's time for Dhuhr, Amina. Let's pray together."

Amina was excited to pray again. She and her Ummi performed wudu and prayed Dhuhr. Amina felt proud that she was learning how to pray.

In the afternoon, Amina's Abu came home. He smiled at Amina and said, "Amina, did you learn about Salah today?"

"Yes, Abu! I learned about Fajr and Dhuhr. Can we pray Asr together?" she asked.

"Of course, Amina," Abu replied. They prayed Asr together, and Abu explained, "Praying helps us stay close to Allah and reminds us to be good and kind."

As the sun began to set, it was time for Maghrib. Amina's older sister, Okhti Layla, joined them for the prayer. "Come, Amina, let's pray Maghrib," Layla said.

Amina felt happy praying with her family. She knew that each prayer was bringing her closer to Allah.

Before bedtime, it was time for Isha, the night prayer. Ummi, Abu, and Layla gathered with Amina to pray. After the prayer, Amina felt calm and ready for bed.

As Amina lay in bed, she thought about her day. She felt proud and happy that she had learned how to pray the five daily prayers. She knew that praying Salah would help her remember Allah and be thankful for all her blessings.

Moral of the Story: Praying Salah helps us remember Allah and be thankful for everything He has given us.

Chapter 6

The Importance of Zakat: Helping Those in Need

One sunny morning, little Amina woke up and greeted her Ummi, "Assalamu Alaikum, Ummi!" Ummi smiled and replied, "Wa Alaikum Assalam, Amina. How are you today?"

Amina hugged her Ummi and said, "Alhamdulillah, I am good, Ummi. What are we going to do today?"

Ummi looked at Amina and said, "Today, we are going to learn about Zakat. Do you know what Zakat is, Amina?"

Amina shook her head, curious. "No, Ummi. What is Zakat?"

Ummi began to explain, "Zakat is one of the five pillars of Islam. It means giving a part of our money to help people who don't have enough. It is very important because it helps us share and be kind."

Just then, Abu came into the room. "Assalamu Alaikum, Amina and Ummi!" he said.

"Wa Alaikum Assalam, Abu!" they replied together. Abu sat down and continued, "Zakat is like a gift from us to those who need it. It helps make sure everyone has enough to eat and live happily."

Amina's eyes lit up. "I want to help too, Abu! How can I do that?"

Abu smiled and said, "You can help by giving some of your toys and clothes that you don't use anymore. There are many children who would be very happy to have them."

Amina ran to her room and gathered some toys and clothes she no longer used. She brought them to Ummi and Abu. "Here, can we give these to the children who need them?" she asked.

Ummi and Abu were very proud of Amina. "Mashallah, Amina! This is a great start. Let's pack these and go visit a family who needs help."

Later, they arrived at the house of a family who needed help. "Assalamu Alaikum," they greeted the family.

"Wa Alaikum Assalam," the family replied warmly. Amina told them about her toys and clothes. The children of the family were very happy to see the toys and clothes. Amina felt very happy too. She saw smiles on their faces and knew she had made a difference.

The next day, Amina was playing outside when she saw her friend, Ali. "Assalamu Alaikum, Ali!" she greeted him.

"Wa Alaikum Assalam, Amina! What are you doing?" he asked.

Amina replied, "I learned about Zakat yesterday. It means helping people who don't have enough. I gave some of my toys and clothes to children who needed them."

Ali smiled and said, "That is very kind of you, Amina! I want to help too. Can I come with you next time?"

"Of course, Ali! We can help together. Bismillah, let's tell our friends about Zakat and how they can help too."

A few days later, Amina and Ali gathered toys and clothes. They went with their parents to give them to children who needed them. The children were very happy and grateful.

Amina felt very proud and happy. She knew that by giving Zakat, she was helping others and making Allah happy. She thanked her Ummi and Abu for teaching her about Zakat.

Moral of the Story: Helping others through Zakat makes Allah happy and helps everyone have what they need.

Chapter 7

Sawm: Fasting During Ramadan

Amina woke up early to the sound of her alarm. She quickly got out of bed and joined her family in the kitchen. "Assalamu Alaikum, Ummi, Abu, and Layla!" she said cheerfully. They all replied together, "Wa Alaikum Assalam, Amina."

Amina sat at the table where a simple meal was prepared. "What are we having for Suhoor?" she asked. Abu answered, "We are having some bread, fruit, and yogurt. It will help us stay strong throughout the day." They all said, "Bismillah," before starting their meal. Amina ate her food and felt ready for the day ahead.

After Suhoor, they prayed Fajr together. Amina felt a sense of peace and closeness with her family and Allah. As the day went on, Amina decided to visit her grandparents. "Ummi, can I go see Jaddi and Jaddati?" she asked. Ummi replied, "Yes, you can, Amina. Remember to be back before Iftar."

Amina walked to her grandparents' house, enjoying the morning sun. "Assalamu Alaikum, Jaddi and Jaddati!" she greeted them. "Wa Alaikum Assalam, Amina," they responded warmly. "How is your fasting going?" Jaddi asked. "It's going well, Alhamdulillah," Amina said. "I'm learning a lot about patience and being thankful."

Jaddi smiled, "That is wonderful, Amina. Fasting is a time for us to grow closer to Allah and to remember those who are less fortunate." Jaddati added, "Would you like to help me prepare some food for Iftar?" Amina eagerly agreed. She loved spending time with her Jaddati in the kitchen. They worked together to make a delicious meal, and as they cooked, Jaddati told Amina stories about Ramadan and how it was celebrated when she was a child.

In the afternoon, Amina walked back home. She was feeling a bit tired but remembered the importance of fasting. She spent some time reading her favorite book and drawing. As the sun began to set, the family gathered in the living room. Ummi and Layla were busy preparing Iftar, and the delicious smells filled the house. Amina helped set the table, placing dates and water for everyone to break their fast.

When it was time for Iftar, Abu said, "Bismillah," and they all took a date. "Alhamdulillah," they said after their first bite. The food tasted even more delicious after a day of fasting. After eating, they prayed Maghrib together. Amina felt grateful for the food and the company of her family. She knew that fasting was a special way to feel closer to Allah and to understand the hardships that others might face.

Later that evening, Amina sat with her family. They talked about their day and what they learned from fasting. Amina shared her experience of helping Jaddati with the Iftar meal and listening to her stories. Abu said, "Fasting during Ramadan teaches us many important lessons, Amina. It reminds us to be patient, kind, and grateful for what we have." Amina nodded, "I understand, Abu. I feel happy and thankful."

As bedtime approached, Amina felt a sense of fulfillment. She knew that each day of fasting brought her closer to her family and Allah. She thanked her Ummi, Abu, and Layla for their support and love.

Moral of the Story: Fasting during Ramadan teaches us patience, gratitude, and empathy for those who have less.

Chapter 8

The Journey of Hajj: Pilgrimage to Mecca

Omar was feeling excited because today was a special day. He eagerly asked, "Ummi, Abu, are we ready to start our journey to Mecca for Hajj?" Abu replied, "Yes, Omar. We are ready. Let's say Bismillah and start our journey." They packed their bags and put on their special clothes called Ihram. Ummi explained, "These clothes show that we are all equal before Allah." As they traveled to Mecca, Omar looked out the window and saw many people heading the same way. "Look, Ummi, so many people are going to Hajj!" he exclaimed. Ummi smiled and said, "Yes, Omar. Muslims from all over the world come to Mecca for Hajj."

When they arrived in Mecca, Omar saw the Kaaba for the first time. "It's so beautiful, Abu!" he said. Abu smiled and said, "Yes, Omar. Now we will walk around the Kaaba seven times. This is called Tawaf." Omar held his parents' hands as they walked around the Kaaba. "This feels very special," he thought.

Next, they went to the hills of Safa and Marwah. Ummi told Omar, "We will walk between these hills seven times. This is called Sa'i. It reminds us of Hajar, the mother of Prophet Ismail, who searched for water for her son." As they walked, Omar thought about Hajar and her strong faith. "She must have been very brave," he said. "Yes, Omar," Abu agreed. "She trusted Allah."

Their journey continued to Mount Arafat. Abu explained, "This is the most important part of Hajj. We will pray and ask Allah for forgiveness here." Omar felt a deep connection to Allah as they prayed together. "I feel very close to Allah," he told his parents.

After Arafat, they went to Muzdalifah, where they slept under the stars and collected small stones. Ummi said, "These stones are for the next ritual." Omar enjoyed looking at the stars and collecting stones. The next day, they went to Mina. Abu said, "We will throw the stones at the pillars. This is called Rami. It reminds us of Prophet Ibrahim and how he rejected the devil." Omar threw his stones carefully, thinking about Prophet Ibrahim. "I feel strong like Prophet Ibrahim," he said. "Alhamdulillah, Omar. You are doing well," Abu replied.

After Rami, they celebrated Eid al-Adha. Ummi explained, "We sacrifice an animal to remember Prophet Ibrahim's willingness to sacrifice for Allah." Omar watched as they shared the meat with those in need. Ummi said, "This is a time of giving and sharing." On their final day in Mecca, they performed Tawaf again. Omar felt happy and peaceful. "I am thankful for this journey, Ummi and Abu," he said. "Alhamdulillah, Omar. Hajj has brought us closer to Allah and each other," Abu replied.

As they prepared to go home, Omar hugged his parents. "Thank you for teaching me about Hajj. I will always remember this journey," he said. "Alhamdulillah, Omar. We are proud of you," Ummi said. On their journey back home, Omar continued to think about everything he had experienced. He remembered the feeling of walking around the Kaaba, the stories of Hajar, and the prayers on Mount Arafat. Each part of Hajj had taught him something new and important. He knew that Hajj was not just a trip, but a journey that would stay with him forever.

Moral of the Story: Hajj teaches us about faith, equality, and the importance of worshiping Allah together.

Chapter 9

Eid al-Fitr: The Festival of Breaking the Fast

The house was buzzing with excitement as everyone prepared for Eid al-Fitr. Omar was helping Ummi in the kitchen, arranging plates of sweets and fresh fruits. "Bismillah," Ummi said as they started preparing a special breakfast. The house smelled wonderful with all the delicious food. Omar helped set the table with dates, sweets, and fresh fruits. "This looks amazing, Ummi," he said.

Abu called out from the living room, "Omar, are you ready for the Eid prayer?" Omar nodded excitedly. "Yes, Abu! I can't wait to celebrate!"

Ummi and Abu smiled. "First, let's get ready," Abu said. Omar put on his new clothes that Ummi had bought for him. They were bright and colorful, perfect for the celebration.

After breakfast, they got ready to go to the mosque for the special Eid prayer. "Come on, Omar," Abu called. "It's time to go." They walked together to the mosque, where they greeted friends and neighbors with "Eid Mubarak!"

The mosque was full of happy people. Omar prayed with his family, feeling thankful for the blessings of Ramadan. "Alhamdulillah," he whispered after the prayer.

After the prayer, everyone hugged and greeted each other. "Eid Mubarak, Akhi!" Omar said to his brother. "Eid Mubarak, Omar!" Akhi replied with a big smile.

They returned home, and the house was soon filled with family members. Omar's grandparents, Jaddi and Jaddati, arrived with gifts. "Assalamu Alaikum, Omar," Jaddi greeted him. "Wa Alaikum Assalam, Jaddi," Omar replied, hugging him tightly.

Jaddi handed Omar a small box. "This is for you," he said. Omar opened it and found a beautiful toy inside. "Thank you, Jaddi! I love it," he exclaimed.

Jaddati brought a tray of sweets. "Here, Omar, try these," she said. Omar took a bite and smiled. "These are delicious, Jaddati. Thank you!"

The house was filled with laughter and joy. Omar and his siblings played games, and everyone enjoyed the special food. Ummi and Jaddati prepared a big feast with biryani, kebabs, and many sweets. "Bismillah," they said as they started eating.

Later in the afternoon, Omar and his family went to visit their neighbors. They brought plates of food and sweets to share. "Assalamu Alaikum, Eid Mubarak!" they greeted their neighbors. "Wa

Alaikum Assalam, Eid Mubarak!" the neighbors replied, welcoming them warmly.

Omar loved seeing the smiles on everyone's faces. He felt happy sharing the joy of Eid with others. They visited many houses, and each time, they were welcomed with hugs and treats.

As the day came to an end, Omar felt grateful for the special time with his family and friends. "Alhamdulillah, this has been the best Eid ever," he said.

Ummi hugged him and said, "Yes, Omar. Eid is a time for joy, family, and community. We are thankful for all our blessings."

Omar smiled and hugged his family. "I love Eid al-Fitr," he said. "I can't wait for next year."

Moral of the Story: Eid al-Fitr is a time for joy, sharing, and being thankful for our blessings.

Chapter 10

Eid al-Adha: The Festival of Sacrifice

Omar was helping his Ummi in the kitchen when he heard Abu call from the living room. "Omar, come here! I want to tell you about Eid al-Adha."

Omar wiped his hands and ran to join Abu. "Assalamu Alaikum, Abu. What is Eid al-Adha?" he asked.

"Wa Alaikum Assalam, Omar," Abu replied with a smile. "Eid al-Adha is a special festival. It is also known as the Festival of Sacrifice. It reminds us of the story of Prophet Ibrahim and his son, Ismail."

Omar sat down next to Abu, eager to listen. "What happened with Prophet Ibrahim and Ismail?" he asked.

"Prophet Ibrahim had a dream in which Allah asked him to sacrifice his son, Ismail, to show his faith and obedience," Abu explained. "Even though it was a difficult test, Prophet Ibrahim was ready to follow Allah's command."

Omar's eyes widened. "Was Ismail afraid?"

"No, Omar," Abu said. "Ismail was very brave and trusted Allah. He told his father to do what Allah had asked. But just as Prophet Ibrahim was about to sacrifice his son, Allah sent a ram to take Ismail's place. Allah was pleased with their faith and obedience."

Omar smiled, feeling proud of Prophet Ibrahim and Ismail. "So, what do we do to remember this story, Abu?"

"On Eid al-Adha, we sacrifice an animal, usually a sheep, goat, or cow, to remember Prophet Ibrahim's willingness to obey Allah," Abu explained. "We share the meat with family, friends, and those in need."

Omar nodded, understanding the importance of the tradition. "What do we do first on Eid al-Adha, Ummi?" he asked as he returned to the kitchen.

"We start the day with a special prayer at the mosque," Ummi said. "Let's get ready."

They all dressed in their best clothes and walked to the mosque. "Eid Mubarak!" they greeted their friends and neighbors.

After the prayer, they returned home, and Abu prepared for the sacrifice. Omar watched as Abu carefully performed the ritual. "Bismillah," Abu said, as he made the sacrifice. "Alhamdulillah," Abu said after the sacrifice was complete. "Now we will share the meat."

Ummi and Abu divided the meat into three parts. "One part is for us, one part is for our relatives, and the last part is for those in need," Ummi explained.

Omar helped pack the meat into bags. "Can we take some to Jaddi and Jaddati?" he asked. "Yes, Omar," Abu replied. "Let's go visit them." They walked to Jaddi and Jaddati's house. "Assalamu Alaikum, Eid Mubarak!" Omar greeted them, "Wa Alaikum Assalam, Eid Mubarak!" Jaddi and Jaddati replied, hugging Omar. "Thank you for bringing the meat. It is very kind of you."

They spent the afternoon visiting relatives and neighbors, sharing the meat and spreading joy. Omar loved seeing the smiles on everyone's faces.

In the evening, they gathered for a big family meal. The table was filled with delicious dishes. "Bismillah," they said together before eating. As they enjoyed the meal, Abu told more stories about Prophet Ibrahim and the significance of Eid al-Adha. Omar listened with wide eyes, feeling grateful for his family and the lessons he was learning.

Moral of the Story: Eid al-Adha teaches us about faith, obedience, and the importance of sharing with others.

Chapter 11

The Significance of the Mosque: A Place of Worship

One bright morning, Omar and his sister, Layla, were playing in the garden when their Ummi called them inside. "Omar, Layla, we are going to visit the mosque today," she said with a warm smile.

Omar's eyes lit up. "What is a mosque, Ummi?" he asked.

"A mosque is a place where we go to pray and worship Allah," Ummi explained. "It is also a place where we learn and spend time with our community." Layla was curious. "Can we see everything there, Ummi?" she asked. "Yes, we will see many things," Ummi replied. "Now let's get ready."

They dressed in their best clothes and set off for the mosque. As they approached, Omar noticed the tall minaret and the beautiful dome. "Look, Layla, it's so big and beautiful!" he exclaimed.

When they entered the mosque, they were greeted with "Assalamu Alaikum" from many people. "Wa Alaikum Assalam," Omar and Layla replied, feeling welcomed.

Ummi led them to the wash area. "Before we pray, we do wudu, a special washing to make us clean," she said. She showed them how to wash their hands, mouth, nose, face, arms, head, and feet. "Bismillah," they said as they began. After wudu, they entered the prayer hall. The floor was covered with soft carpets, and there was a calm, peaceful atmosphere. "This is where we pray," Ummi whispered. "We will join the others for the Dhuhr prayer."

They found a spot, and Ummi showed Omar and Layla how to stand, bow, and prostrate during the prayer. Omar tried to copy Ummi's movements, feeling peaceful as he did.

After the prayer, Ummi took them to a room where children were learning about Islam. "This is where we learn more about our faith," she said.

A friendly teacher welcomed them. "Assalamu Alaikum, Omar and Layla. Would you like to join us?" she asked. "Wa Alaikum Assalam," they replied, excited to join the class. The teacher told them stories about the prophets and taught them important lessons about kindness and helping others. Omar and Layla listened carefully and enjoyed the stories.

After the class, they rejoined Ummi, who was talking to other women. "What did you learn, Omar?" she asked. "I learned about the prophets and how to be kind," Omar said proudly. "That's wonderful, Omar," Ummi said. "The mosque is not just a place to pray, but also a place to learn."

Later, they went to a large room where people were sharing food and talking. "The mosque is also a place where we come together as a community," Ummi explained. "We support each other and share our joys and challenges." Omar and Layla saw people laughing and talking, sharing food and stories. They even made some new friends. As they left the mosque, Omar felt happy and peaceful.

On the way home, Layla said, "I really liked visiting the mosque, Ummi. Can we come back again?" "Of course, Layla," Ummi replied. "The mosque is always open for us to pray, learn, and be with our community."

Omar hugged Ummi and said, "Thank you for taking us to the mosque. I learned so much today." "Alhamdulillah," Ummi said. "I am glad you both enjoyed it. The mosque is an important part of our lives." Omar and Layla smiled, feeling grateful for the special visit. They couldn't wait to go back and learn more.

Moral of the Story: The mosque is a special place where we pray, learn, and come together as a community.

Chapter 12

Learning Wudu: The Ablution Before Prayer

LEARNING WUDU: THE ABLUTION BEFORE PRAYER

Omar was playing in the garden when his Ummi called him inside. "Omar, come here! It's time to learn something important." Omar ran inside, curious to know what it was. "Assalamu Alaikum, Ummi," he greeted her. "Wa Alaikum Assalam, Omar," Ummi replied with a smile. "Today, we will learn how to do Wudu. It is the special washing we do before we pray to Allah."

Omar was excited. "What do we do first, Ummi?" he asked. Ummi took him to the sink and said, "First, we say Bismillah. This means 'In the name of Allah.'" They both said "Bismillah" together. "Now, we wash our hands," Ummi said. She showed Omar how to wash his hands up to the wrists three times. Omar copied her, enjoying the feel of the cool water.

Next, Ummi explained, "We rinse our mouth three times." She took a handful of water, rinsed her mouth, and spit it out. Omar did the same. "This is fun, Ummi!" he said with a giggle. "Now, we clean our nose," Ummi continued. "We take a little water in our hand, sniff it gently into our nose, and blow it out. We do this three times." Omar followed her instructions carefully.

"Next, we wash our face," Ummi said, splashing water on her face. She made sure to cover her entire face from her forehead to her chin.

Omar loved splashing the water and made sure to cover his whole face too. "Now, we wash our arms," Ummi said. "We start with the right arm, washing from the fingertips to the elbow three times, then do the same with the left arm." Omar watched carefully and did just as Ummi showed him.

Ummi then said, "Next, we wipe our head. We wet our hands and pass them over our head from the front to the back and back to the front." Omar did this and felt the coolness on his head. "Now, we clean our ears," Ummi said. "We use our wet fingers to wipe inside and behind our ears." Omar cleaned his ears and giggled because it tickled a little.

"Lastly, we wash our feet," Ummi explained. "We wash our right foot from the toes to the ankle three times, then the left foot." Omar followed along, making sure to wash between his toes. "And that's how we do Wudu!" Ummi said proudly.

Omar felt happy and clean. "Alhamdulillah, Ummi! I feel ready to pray now." Ummi smiled and said, "Alhamdulillah, Omar. You did a great job. Wudu helps us be clean and ready to talk to Allah."

Later that day, Abu came home. Omar ran to him and said, "Assalamu Alaikum, Abu! I learned how to do Wudu today!" Abu hugged him and replied, "Wa Alaikum Assalam, Omar! That is wonderful. Show me how you do it." Omar eagerly showed Abu each step of Wudu, and Abu praised him for doing it correctly.

In the evening, the family gathered to pray together. Omar felt proud and confident as he performed Wudu and joined his family in prayer. He knew that being clean and ready was an important part of praying to Allah.

After the prayer, Ummi said, "Omar, you did very well today. I am proud of you." Omar smiled and said, "Thank you, Ummi. I am happy I learned how to do Wudu. Now I can always be ready to pray."

Moral of the Story: Wudu helps us be clean and ready to pray to Allah.

Chapter 13

The Call to Prayer: Adhan

Omar was playing with his sister, Layla, in the living room when they heard a beautiful sound coming from the mosque nearby. "Ummi, what is that sound?" Omar asked, looking curious.

Ummi smiled and said, "That is the Adhan, Omar. It is the call to prayer. It tells us it is time to pray."

Omar listened carefully. "What does the Adhan mean, Ummi?" he asked.

Ummi sat down with Omar and Layla. "The Adhan has special words that invite Muslims to come to the mosque and pray. It starts with 'Allahu Akbar,' which means 'Allah is the Greatest.' Then it says, 'Ashhadu an la ilaha illa Allah,' which means 'I bear witness that there is no god but Allah.'"

Omar and Layla listened with wide eyes. Ummi continued, "The Adhan also says, 'Ashhadu anna Muhammadan Rasool Allah,' which means 'I bear witness that Muhammad is the Messenger of Allah.' Then it invites us to prayer with 'Hayya 'ala as-Salah,' which means 'Come to prayer,' and 'Hayya 'ala al-Falah,' which means 'Come to success.' Finally, it ends with 'Allahu Akbar, Allahu Akbar, la ilaha illa Allah.'"

Layla looked up at Ummi and asked, "Ummi, why do we have the Adhan?"

Ummi explained, "The Adhan reminds us to take a break from our activities and pray to Allah. It helps us remember that prayer is very important in our lives. The person who calls the Adhan is called a muezzin. He stands in a high place so that everyone can hear the call."

Just then, Abu came home. Omar ran to him and said, "Assalamu Alaikum, Abu! We were learning about the Adhan."

"Wa Alaikum Assalam, Omar," Abu replied, giving him a hug. "The Adhan is very special. It brings the community together for prayer."

Ummi suggested, "Let's go to the mosque to hear the Adhan up close and pray together." Omar and Layla were excited. "Yes, let's go!" they said.

As they walked to the mosque, Omar saw the tall minaret. "Is that where the muezzin calls the Adhan?" he asked.

"Yes, Omar," Abu said. "The minaret is tall so the sound can travel far, and everyone can hear it."

When they arrived at the mosque, they heard the muezzin call the Adhan. The sound was clear and beautiful. "Allahu Akbar, Allahu Akbar," the muezzin called. Omar felt a sense of peace listening to the call.

They performed Wudu and entered the prayer hall. Omar saw many people coming together to pray. "The Adhan brings us all together," Abu said. "It is a reminder of the importance of prayer and our faith."

After the prayer, Omar felt happy and calm. "Alhamdulillah, I like hearing the Adhan and praying with everyone," he said. Abu smiled and said, "Alhamdulillah, Omar. The Adhan is a gift from Allah. It helps us remember to pray and stay connected to our community and faith."

On their way home, Omar held Abu's hand and said, "Thank you for teaching me about the Adhan. I will always listen carefully and remember to pray."

Layla added, "Me too, Ummi. I love the Adhan. It sounds so beautiful." Ummi hugged them both and said, "I am glad you both learned about the Adhan. It is an important part of our lives as Muslims."

Moral of the Story: The Adhan reminds us of the importance of prayer and brings the community together.

Chapter 14

The Beauty of Islamic Art and Calligraphy

Omar loved to draw and paint. One day, while he was coloring a picture, his Ummi came over and said, "Omar, would you like to learn about Islamic art and calligraphy?" Omar's eyes lit up with excitement. "Yes, Ummi! I would love that!" he replied.

Ummi led Omar to the living room, where she had set up some art supplies. "Islamic art is very special," Ummi explained. "It often uses beautiful patterns and designs, and calligraphy, which is the art of beautiful writing, is an important part of it."

Omar looked at the paper and pens Ummi had laid out. "What do we do first?" he asked eagerly. Ummi smiled and said, "First, we say Bismillah, and then we can start by learning some simple shapes and patterns."

They both said, "Bismillah," and Ummi began to show Omar how to draw different geometric shapes. "These shapes are often used in Islamic art to create beautiful patterns," she said. Omar tried his best to copy the shapes, feeling proud when his patterns looked nice.

Next, Ummi brought out a special pen for calligraphy. "This is a calligraphy pen," she said. "It helps us write in a beautiful way." She showed Omar how to hold the pen and make flowing, graceful letters.

"Let's start with 'Alhamdulillah,'" Ummi suggested, which means 'All praise is due to Allah.'

Omar carefully watched Ummi as she wrote the word in beautiful Arabic script. Then he tried it himself, his tongue sticking out in concentration. "Alhamdulillah," he said softly as he finished his first word. Ummi smiled proudly. "You did a great job, Omar! Calligraphy takes practice, but you are doing very well."

They continued practicing different words and phrases, and Omar learned how to write "Bismillah" and "Assalamu Alaikum." He loved seeing how the letters flowed together to make beautiful words.

Later that day, Abu came home and saw Omar's artwork. "Assalamu Alaikum, Omar! These are wonderful!" he exclaimed. Omar beamed with pride. "Wa Alaikum Assalam, Abu. Ummi taught me about Islamic art and calligraphy today."

Abu sat down next to Omar and said, "Islamic art and calligraphy are very special. They help us express our faith and make beautiful things to praise Allah." Omar nodded, feeling happy to learn something so important.

The next day, Ummi took Omar to visit his Jaddi and Jaddati. "Assalamu Alaikum, Jaddi and Jaddati," Omar greeted them. "Wa Alaikum Assalam, Omar," they replied warmly. Omar showed them his calligraphy and patterns. "Mashallah, these are beautiful," Jaddi said. "Islamic art has a long history, and it's wonderful to see you learning it."

Jaddati added, "In our culture, creating art is a way to show our love for Allah and to beautify our surroundings." Omar felt proud and inspired to keep practicing.

As the days went by, Omar spent more time drawing and practicing calligraphy. He loved creating beautiful patterns and writing special words. He knew that through his art, he could show his love for Allah and share beauty with others.

One evening, as Omar was finishing a new piece of calligraphy, he said, "Alhamdulillah, I am so happy to learn about Islamic art. Thank you, Ummi and Abu, for teaching me." Ummi hugged him and said, "We are proud of you, Omar. Keep practicing and always remember that your art is a beautiful way to praise Allah."

Moral of the Story: Islamic art and calligraphy help us express our faith and create beauty to praise Allah.

Chapter 15

Understanding Halal and Haram

Omar was playing in the garden when he heard his Ummi calling him. "Omar, come inside! It's time for lunch." Omar ran into the house, excited to see what Ummi had prepared. "Assalamu Alaikum, Ummi!" he greeted her. "Wa Alaikum Assalam, Omar," Ummi replied with a smile. "Today, we are having chicken and vegetables for lunch. But before we eat, I want to teach you something important."

Omar looked curious. "What is it, Ummi?" he asked. Ummi sat down with Omar at the kitchen table. "Omar, do you know what Halal and Haram mean?" she asked.

Omar shook his head. "No, Ummi. What do they mean?" Ummi explained, "Halal means things that are allowed for us to eat and do. Haram means things that are not allowed. It is important for us to know the difference so we can follow what Allah wants."

Omar listened carefully. "Can you give me an example, Ummi?" he asked. "Of course," Ummi said. "This chicken we are having for lunch is Halal because it was prepared in a way that is allowed. But there are some foods, like pork, that are Haram and we should not eat them."

Omar nodded, starting to understand. "So, Halal is good and Haram is not good?" he asked. "That's right, Omar," Ummi said. "And it's not just about food. There are also actions that are Halal and Haram.

For example, being kind to others and telling the truth are Halal. But hurting someone or telling lies are Haram."

Just then, Abu came home from work. "Assalamu Alaikum, Abu!" Omar greeted him. "Wa Alaikum Assalam, Omar," Abu replied, giving him a hug. "What are you learning about today?" "Ummi is teaching me about Halal and Haram," Omar said proudly. "That is very important, Omar," Abu said. "Knowing what is Halal and Haram helps us live in a way that pleases Allah."

Ummi brought the food to the table, and they all said "Bismillah" before starting to eat. As they enjoyed their meal, Omar thought more about what he had learned.

After lunch, Omar saw his sister, Layla, playing with her toys. "Assalamu Alaikum, Layla!" he said. "Wa Alaikum Assalam, Omar!" she replied.

"Do you know what Halal and Haram mean?" Omar asked her. Layla shook her head. "No, what do they mean?"

Omar explained, "Halal means things that are allowed, and Haram means things that are not allowed. Ummi and Abu said it's important to know the difference."

Layla looked thoughtful. "So, what we eat and how we act can be Halal or Haram?" she asked. "Yes," Omar said. "Like eating chicken is Halal, but eating pork is Haram. And being kind is Halal, but being mean is Haram."

Layla smiled. "I want to do more Halal things," she said. Omar nodded. "Me too, Layla. Let's always try to do what is right."

In the evening, the family gathered for dinner. Omar felt happy knowing more about Halal and Haram. He knew that understanding these things would help him make good choices.

After dinner, Omar said, "Ummi, Abu, can we always talk about what is Halal and Haram so we can remember to do the right things?" Abu nodded and said, "Of course, Omar. We will always help each other make good choices."

Omar smiled and felt peaceful. "Alhamdulillah, I am glad we can learn together," he said.

Ummi hugged him and said, "We are proud of you, Omar. You are learning to make choices that please Allah."

Moral of the Story: Knowing what is Halal and Haram helps us make good choices and live in a way that pleases Allah.

Chapter 16

The Quranic Stories: Lessons for Life

Omar and his sister Layla were excited as they sat down with their grandfather, Jaddi, in the garden. "Assalamu Alaikum, Jaddi," they greeted him. "Wa Alaikum Assalam, my dear ones," Jaddi replied warmly. "Today, I will share with you some wonderful stories from the Quran."

Omar and Layla loved listening to Jaddi's stories. "What are we going to learn today, Jaddi?" asked Omar.

Jaddi smiled and began, "Let's start with the story of Prophet Nuh. Allah asked Prophet Nuh to build a big boat, called an ark, because a great flood was coming. Prophet Nuh listened to Allah and built the ark. He took his family and many animals with him on the ark. When the flood came, they were all safe. This story teaches us to always listen to Allah and trust His guidance."

Layla's eyes sparkled with interest. "That sounds amazing, Jaddi. Prophet Nuh was very wise to listen to Allah," she said.

"Indeed, Layla," Jaddi replied. "Now, let me tell you the story of Prophet Sulaiman. He was a very wise king and could talk to animals. One day, a little ant warned its friends to hide because Prophet Sulaiman's army was coming. Prophet Sulaiman heard the ant and smiled. He was kind and careful not to harm the ants. This story teaches us to be kind to all creatures and to be wise."

Omar nodded thoughtfully. "Prophet Sulaiman was very kind and wise," he said.

"Yes, Omar," Jaddi continued. "Next, let's hear about Prophet Yunus. He was swallowed by a big fish because he tried to run away from what Allah asked him to do. While inside the fish, Prophet Yunus prayed to Allah and asked for forgiveness. Allah forgave him, and the fish released him. This story teaches us that we should always obey Allah and ask for forgiveness when we make mistakes."

Layla was amazed. "Being inside a fish must have been so scary, but Prophet Yunus kept praying," she said.

"Exactly, Layla," Jaddi said. "He never lost hope. Now, for the last story today, we have Prophet Isa. He performed many miracles with Allah's help. He healed the sick and brought comfort to those in need. Prophet Isa taught people about love and kindness. This story teaches us to always help others and be kind."

Omar and Layla listened intently. "Prophet Isa was very loving and helpful," Omar said.

"Yes, he was," Jaddi replied. "The stories of the prophets in the Quran teach us many important lessons. They show us how to live a good and meaningful life."

As the sun began to set, Ummi came to call them for dinner. "Bismillah, let's go eat," she said. "Thank you, Jaddi, for the wonderful stories," Omar and Layla said as they hugged him.

"Alhamdulillah, I am glad you enjoyed them," Jaddi said. "Remember, the lessons from these stories are very important."

During dinner, Omar and Layla shared the stories they had learned with their parents. Abu smiled and said, "These stories from the Quran are not just tales; they guide us in our everyday lives."

That night, Omar and Layla talked about the stories before going to sleep. "Let's always be kind, wise, and trust Allah," Omar said.

"Yes, and let's never lose hope and always help others," Layla added.

They fell asleep feeling happy and inspired, knowing the lessons from the Quran would help them become better people.

Moral of the Story: The stories from the Quran teach us to listen to Allah, be kind, wise, and always help others.

Chapter 17

The Significance of the Hijab

THE SIGNIFICANCE OF THE HIJAB

Layla was sitting in the living room with her Ummi when she saw a beautiful scarf on the table. "Ummi, what is this scarf for?" she asked curiously.

Ummi smiled and said, "Layla, this is a hijab. It is a special scarf that Muslim girls and women wear to cover their hair. Would you like to learn more about it?"

Layla nodded eagerly. "Yes, Ummi, please tell me more!"

Ummi began, "The hijab is a sign of modesty and respect. It shows that we are proud of our faith and that we want to be seen for who we are, not just for how we look. Wearing the hijab is a personal choice, and it helps us feel closer to Allah."

Layla listened carefully. "Ummi, can I try wearing the hijab?" she asked.

"Of course, Layla," Ummi replied. She gently placed the hijab on Layla's head and adjusted it so it fit perfectly. Layla looked at herself in the mirror and smiled. "I like it, Ummi. It feels special."

Just then, Layla's father, Abu, came into the room. "Assalamu Alaikum, Layla. You look beautiful in your hijab," he said.

"Wa Alaikum Assalam, Abu. Thank you," Layla replied, feeling proud.

Abu sat down with them and said, "Layla, wearing the hijab is a wonderful way to show your love for Allah. It is also a way to show respect for yourself and others."

Layla nodded. "I want to wear the hijab, Abu. I feel happy wearing it."

Later that day, Layla went to visit her grandmother, Jaddati. "Assalamu Alaikum, Jaddati," she greeted her.

"Wa Alaikum Assalam, Layla," Jaddati replied, giving her a warm hug. "I see you are wearing a hijab. It looks lovely on you."

"Thank you, Jaddati. Ummi and Abu taught me about the hijab, and I decided to wear it," Layla said proudly.

Jaddati smiled and said, "The hijab is a beautiful way to show your faith and modesty. It also shows that you are proud to be a Muslim."

In the evening, Layla played with her brother, Akhi Omar. "Assalamu Alaikum, Layla. You look nice in your hijab," Omar said.

"Wa Alaikum Assalam, Akhi. Thank you," Layla replied. She felt happy knowing that her family supported her decision.

Before bedtime, Layla sat with her Ummi and Abu. "Ummi, Abu, thank you for teaching me about the hijab. I feel proud and happy wearing it," she said.

"Alhamdulillah, Layla. We are proud of you for making this choice," Ummi said, hugging her.

Abu added, "Always remember, Layla, wearing the hijab is a way to show your love for Allah and your respect for yourself and others. It is a special part of our faith."

Layla smiled and said, "I will always remember that, Abu. I love wearing my hijab."

That night, as Layla went to bed, she felt a sense of peace and happiness. She knew that wearing the hijab was a special way to show her faith and love for Allah.

Moral of the Story: Wearing the hijab is a way to show your faith, modesty, and respect for yourself and others.

Chapter 18

Jannah: The Gardens of Paradise

Amina was playing with her dolls in the living room when her grandfather, Jaddi, called her over. "Amina, come sit with me for a moment," he said gently.

"Assalamu Alaikum, Jaddi," Amina greeted him as she climbed onto his lap. "Wa Alaikum Assalam, my dear Amina," Jaddi replied, giving her a warm hug. "Today, I want to tell you about Jannah, the Gardens of Paradise."

Amina's eyes sparkled with curiosity. "What is Jannah, Jaddi?" she asked.

"Jannah is a beautiful place that Allah has created for those who do good deeds and follow His guidance," Jaddi began. "In Jannah, there are rivers of milk, honey, and pure water. There are also fruits of all kinds, more delicious than anything we have ever tasted."

Amina imagined the delicious fruits and asked, "What else is in Jannah, Jaddi?"

"There are palaces made of gold and silver," Jaddi continued. "The houses in Jannah are more beautiful than anything we can imagine. Each person will have their own palace, and it will be perfect for them."

Amina smiled, thinking of her own palace. "Can we play in Jannah, Jaddi?" she asked.

"Yes, Amina," Jaddi said with a chuckle. "In Jannah, you can play and be happy all the time. There are beautiful gardens where you can run and play. There are also animals that you can talk to and be friends with. The birds in Jannah sing the sweetest songs." Amina clapped her hands in delight. "I want to go to Jannah, Jaddi!" she exclaimed.

"Alhamdulillah, Amina," Jaddi said. "To go to Jannah, we must always try to be good, pray to Allah, and be kind to others. Allah loves those who do good deeds."

Amina nodded, understanding the importance of being good. "What else can we do in Jannah, Jaddi?" she asked. "In Jannah, we can meet the prophets and righteous people," Jaddi said. "We can talk to them and learn from their wisdom. We can also see our loved ones who have passed away and be with them forever."

Amina felt happy hearing this. "I want to be with you in Jannah, Jaddi," she said. "Inshallah, Amina," Jaddi replied. "If we live our lives following Allah's guidance, we will all be together in Jannah."

Later that day, Amina shared what she had learned with her brother, Akhi Omar. "Assalamu Alaikum, Omar. Do you know about Jannah?" she asked. "Wa Alaikum Assalam, Amina. What did Jaddi tell you?" Omar replied.

"Jaddi said Jannah is the most beautiful garden with rivers of milk and honey," Amina explained. "There are palaces made of gold and silver, and we can play and be happy all the time." Omar smiled and said, "That sounds wonderful, Amina. I want to go to Jannah too. We should always try to do good deeds and pray to Allah."

Amina agreed. "Yes, Omar. We should be kind and help others."

In the evening, Amina and Omar shared what they had learned with their parents during dinner. Ummi replied. "Jannah is indeed a beautiful place. Always remember to do good deeds and pray to Allah." Abu added, "If we follow Allah's guidance and are kind to others, we will all be together in Jannah."

Amina and Omar felt happy and peaceful knowing about Jannah. They promised to always try their best to be good and kind.

Moral of the Story: To enter Jannah, we must do good deeds, be kind, and follow Allah's guidance.

Chapter 19

Family Love in Islam

Fatima woke up early in the morning to the sound of birds chirping outside her window. She whispered, "Bismillah," as she got out of bed. Today was a special day because her Jaddi and Jaddati were coming to visit. Fatima loved her grandparents very much and couldn't wait to see them.

Fatima's Ummi was in the kitchen making breakfast. "Assalamu Alaikum, Ummi," Fatima greeted her mother. "Wa Alaikum Assalam, Yumma," her mother replied with a smile. The delicious smell of pancakes filled the air. "Bismillah," Fatima said before taking her first bite.

After breakfast, Fatima helped her Ummi tidy up the house. She dusted the furniture and arranged the cushions on the sofa. Her Akhi, Ali, was helping their Abu in the garden. "Khuya, can you help me with this?" Fatima called out to her brother. "Of course, Ikht," Ali replied, always happy to help his little sister.

Soon, the doorbell rang. "They're here!" Fatima shouted excitedly. She ran to the door and opened it to see her Jaddi and Jaddati standing there with big smiles. "Assalamu Alaikum, Jaddi! Assalamu Alaikum, Jaddati!" Fatima greeted them. "Wa Alaikum Assalam, my dear," they replied, hugging her tightly.

Fatima's Baba came to greet them too. "Welcome, welcome," he said. The whole family gathered in the living room, sharing stories and laughing together. Fatima loved listening to her Jaddi's stories about when he was young. He told them about his adventures and how important family is in Islam.

"Family is a gift from Allah," Jaddi said. "We must always be kind and loving to each other. Alhamdulillah, we are together today." Fatima nodded, understanding how special her family was.

Later, Fatima and her Ukhti, Aisha, decided to make a card for their Jaddati. They used colorful paper and markers to draw beautiful flowers and hearts. "Jaddati will love this," Aisha said. "Yes, she will, Okhti," Fatima agreed. They wrote a message inside the card: "Thank you for always loving us, Jaddati. We love you very much."

When they gave the card to their Jaddati, her eyes filled with tears of joy. "Shukran, my lovely granddaughters," she said, hugging them tightly. Fatima felt warm inside, happy to see her Jaddati so happy.

In the evening, the family gathered for dinner. "Bismillah," they said before starting their meal. They shared stories, laughed, and enjoyed the delicious food that Ummi had prepared. Fatima felt so grateful to have her family around her.

After dinner, Fatima's Jaddi told them more stories about how important it is to respect and love one another. "In Islam, family is very important," he said. "We must always be there for each other, through good times and hard times."

As the night came to an end, Fatima felt very tired but also very happy. She hugged her Jaddi and Jaddati goodnight. "Goodnight, Jaddi. Goodnight, Jaddati," she said. "Goodnight, my dear Fatima," they replied.

Before going to bed, Fatima whispered, "Alhamdulillah," thanking Allah for her wonderful family. She knew that with love and respect, her family would always be strong.

Moral of the Story: Family is very important in Islam. We must always love, respect, and help each other.

Chapter 20

The Role of the Imam: A Leader in the Community

Every morning, Omar woke up early, excited to start the day. He whispered, "Alhamdulillah," as he got out of bed, thankful for a new day. Today was special because he was going to the mosque with his Abu. Omar loved going to the mosque. It was a place where he felt happy and peaceful.

When they arrived, Abu said, "Assalamu Alaikum" to everyone they met. Omar repeated, "Assalamu Alaikum," and everyone smiled at him. They went inside the mosque and saw the Imam. The Imam was a very kind and wise man. He always had a smile on his face and kind words for everyone.

"Assalamu Alaikum, Imam," Abu greeted him. The Imam replied, "Wa Alaikum Assalam," and patted Omar on the head. Omar felt proud to be noticed by the Imam.

The Imam began to speak to the people in the mosque. He told them stories from the Quran and taught them how to pray. Omar listened carefully, trying to remember everything. The Imam's voice was gentle and calming. After the prayers, the Imam sat with the children. "Do you know why we say 'Alhamdulillah' when we wake up?" he asked. Omar raised his hand excitedly. "Yes, it means 'All praise is for Allah,'" he said. The Imam smiled and said, "That's right, Omar. It helps us remember to be thankful for everything Allah has given us."

Later, the Imam walked around the community. He visited the sick and the elderly, bringing them comfort and cheer. He always had kind words and helpful advice. Omar noticed how everyone respected the Imam and listened to him.

One day, Omar and his family went to a community event at the mosque. There were many people there, all helping each other and having fun. The Imam was there too, making sure everyone was happy and that everything was going well. "Omar, come here," called his Ummi. Omar ran to her and saw the Imam talking to his Jaddi and Jaddati. They were smiling and laughing together. Omar loved seeing his grandparents happy. The Imam saw Omar and said, "Assalamu Alaikum, Omar. Are you having a good time?" Omar nodded and said, "Alhamdulillah, yes, I am!"

The Imam asked the children to sit in a circle. "Today, we will learn about gratitude," he said. He told them a story about a boy who always thanked Allah for everything he had, even the small things. The children listened carefully and promised to always be thankful. When it was time to leave, Omar felt sad. He didn't want the day to end. But the Imam reminded him, "You can always come back to the mosque. It's a place for everyone to learn and be together." Omar smiled and said, "Inshallah, I will come back soon!"

At home, Omar told his sister, Aisha, about his day. "The Imam is like a guide," he explained. "He helps us understand Allah's words and shows us how to be good." Aisha listened and said, "I want to go to the mosque too and learn from the Imam!" That evening, Omar and Aisha decided to make a special dua (prayer) for the Imam. They sat down with their Ummi and Abu and asked Allah to bless the Imam for all his kindness and teachings. "Oh Allah, please bless our Imam and keep him healthy and happy," they prayed together.

The next day, Omar and Aisha saw the Imam at the mosque again. "Imam, we made a special dua for you," Omar said. The Imam's eyes twinkled with joy. "Shukran, my dear children," he said, giving them a warm hug. "Your dua means so much to me."

Omar felt happy and peaceful. He knew that the Imam was a special person who helped everyone in the community. He promised to always listen to the Imam and be thankful for everything he had.

Moral of the Story: Always listen to your Imam and be thankful for everything you have.

Chapter 21

Sami's Path to Taqwa

Sami was a cheerful boy who lived in a cozy house with his Ummi, Baba, and little brother, Khuya. Every morning, Ummi would remind Sami, "Remember to say Bismillah before you start your day, Sami." Sami would smile and say, "Yes, Ummi! Bismillah!" He knew it was important to start his day with Allah's name.

It was a sunny day, Sami and Khuya decided to play outside. As they were playing, they saw their neighbor, Jaddati, trying to carry heavy bags of groceries. Sami quickly ran to her and said, "Let me help you, Jaddati." Jaddati smiled and said, "Thank you, Sami. You are a kind boy." Sami felt happy helping her, remembering that Allah loves those who are kind. This was his first step in understanding taqwa, the consciousness of Allah in his actions.

Later that day, Sami and Khuya went to the park. They saw a group of kids throwing stones at birds. Sami remembered what Baba had told him, "Sami, Allah loves all His creations. We should never harm them." So, Sami went up to the kids and said, "Please stop hurting the birds. Allah is watching us, and we should be kind to all creatures." The kids listened to Sami and stopped throwing stones. Sami felt proud, knowing he was practicing taqwa by being mindful of Allah's presence.

In the afternoon, Sami and Khuya helped Ummi in the kitchen. Ummi was making a big meal for the family. She said, "Sami, always remember to thank Allah for the food we have. Many people are not as fortunate." Sami nodded and said, "Alhamdulillah for the food we have." He helped set the table, feeling grateful and aware of Allah's blessings. This made him understand that taqwa also means being thankful for everything Allah has given.

The next day, Sami found some money on the ground while walking to school. He picked it up and thought, "I could keep this, but that wouldn't be right." He remembered what Baba always said, "Sami, be honest and fair. Allah sees everything we do." So, Sami took the money to his teacher and said, "I found this outside. Someone might be looking for it." The teacher smiled and said, "Thank you, Sami. You did the right thing." Sami felt happy, knowing he was practicing taqwa by being honest and fair.

One evening, Sami and his family visited Jaddi. Jaddi greeted them warmly, "As-salamu alaykum, my dear ones." They spent the evening talking about the importance of being mindful of Allah. Jaddi said, "Sami, taqwa means being aware of Allah in everything you do, whether big or small. It means remembering that Allah is always watching and trying to do what pleases Him."

Sami listened carefully, realizing that taqwa was about more than just big actions. It was about the small, everyday choices he made. It was about being kind, honest, and grateful, and always remembering Allah.

The next day at school, Sami saw his friend Ahmed looking sad. Sami asked, "As-salamu alaykum, Ahmed. What's wrong?" Ahmed replied, "Wa alaykum as-salam. I lost my notebook, and I can't find it." Sami decided to help Ahmed. They searched everywhere and finally found the notebook under a bench. Ahmed smiled and said, "Alhamdulillah! Thank you, Sami." Sami felt happy helping his friend, knowing he was practicing taqwa by being helpful and caring.

Before going to bed that night, Sami prayed. He thanked Allah for guiding him and helping him understand taqwa. He promised to always be mindful of Allah in his actions and thoughts. Sami knew that practicing taqwa made him a better person and brought him closer to Allah.

Moral of the Story: Always be aware of Allah in your actions and thoughts, and try to be kind, honest, and grateful every day.

Chapter 22

Sami Learns Patience: Sabr

In a small village surrounded by green fields, a kind boy named Sami lived with his family. Sami's family included his Ummi, Baba, and little sister, Ukhti. One sunny morning, Sami was eager to go outside and play. As he was about to run out the door, Baba gently reminded him, "Sami, don't forget to say Bismillah before you start your day."

Sami stopped, smiled, and said, "Bismillah!" He knew it was important to start his day with Allah's name.

Sami loved to play outside. One day, he planted a small seed in the garden. He watered it and waited for it to grow. Every day, Sami checked the spot where he planted the seed. He hoped to see a sprout, but nothing happened. Sami felt sad and told Baba, "I water the seed every day, but it doesn't grow."

Baba smiled and said, "Sami, you need to have sabr. Sabr means patience. Sometimes good things take time. Keep caring for your seed, and insha'Allah, it will grow." Sami nodded, understanding that he needed to be patient.

One afternoon, Sami and Ukhti were playing with a kite. The kite got stuck in a tree. Sami tried to pull it down, but it was too high. He felt frustrated and said, "I can't get it down, Ummi!" Ummi came to him and said, "Sami, remember to have sabr. Let's think of a way to solve the problem."

Sami took a deep breath and thought. He found a long stick and carefully used it to pull the kite from the tree. It took a few tries, but finally, the kite came down. Sami smiled and said, "Alhamdulillah! I did it!" He felt happy that his patience had helped him.

A few weeks later, Sami noticed something green in the garden. His seed had finally sprouted! He ran to Baba and said, "Baba, look! The seed is growing!" Baba hugged him and said, "See, Sami? Your sabr paid off. Good things come to those who wait."

One day, Sami and his family went to visit Jaddi. Jaddi loved to tell stories. He said, "Sami, let me tell you a story about patience. Once, there was a farmer who planted a tree. He watered it every day and waited for it to bear fruit. It took many years, but the farmer never gave up. One day, the tree was full of fruits. The farmer was very happy because his sabr was rewarded."

Sami listened carefully, understanding that patience was important in many things. He thanked Jaddi and promised to always remember the lesson of sabr.

One evening, Sami and Ukhti were making a puzzle. It was a big puzzle, and some pieces were hard to find. Sami felt frustrated again. Ukhti said, "Sami, let's have sabr and keep looking. We will find the pieces." Sami smiled at Ukhti's words. They continued working on the puzzle, and after a while, they finished it. Sami felt proud and said, "We did it, Ukhti! Alhamdulillah!"

Before bed, Sami prayed and thanked Allah for teaching him the value of sabr. He promised to always try to be patient in difficult times. He knew that sabr made him stronger and happier.

Sami understood that sabr was not just about waiting but also about trusting Allah and staying positive. He felt closer to Allah and more confident each day as he continued to practice patience in his life.

Moral of the Story: Always be patient and trust that good things will come in time.

Chapter 23

Adab: The Magic of Good Manners

Fatima was a kind and cheerful girl who lived in a small village with her family. She loved playing with her friends and helping her Ummi and Abu at home. One sunny morning, Fatima woke up with a big smile. She said, "Bismillah," which means "In the name of Allah," and got ready for the day. Her Ummi, always loving and gentle, smiled back and said, "Assalamu Alaikum, Fatima!"

"Wa Alaikum Assalam, Ummi!" Fatima replied. She went to the living room and saw her little brother, Ali, playing with his toys. "Assalamu Alaikum, Akhi!" she greeted him.

"Wa Alaikum Assalam, Ukhti!" Ali replied with a grin.

Fatima helped her Ummi tidy up the house. As they were cleaning, their neighbor, Mr. Hasan, knocked on the door. Fatima opened it and said, "Assalamu Alaikum, Mr. Hasan. How can we help you?"

"Wa Alaikum Assalam, Fatima," Mr. Hasan replied. "I need some help moving a table. Could you ask your Abu to assist me?"

Fatima ran to her Abu and explained the situation. Her Abu went to help Mr. Hasan, and Fatima followed to see if she could be of assistance. She held the door open and helped move small items. Mr. Hasan smiled and said, "Thank you, Fatima. You have very good adab."

Later that day, Fatima and her family went to visit her grandmother, Jaddati, who lived nearby. When they arrived, Fatima ran to her and said, "Assalamu Alaikum, Jaddati!"

"Wa Alaikum Assalam, my dear Fatima," Jaddati replied, giving her a warm hug.

Fatima noticed that Jaddati looked tired. "Can I help you with anything, Jaddati?" she asked.

"Thank you, Fatima. Could you help me water the plants in the garden?" Jaddati asked.

Fatima happily agreed and went to the garden. She carefully watered the plants, making sure not to spill too much water. When she finished, Jaddati said, "You did a wonderful job, Fatima. You are very helpful and kind."

In the evening, Fatima's family gathered for dinner at Jaddati's house. Before they ate, Fatima's Abu reminded everyone, "Remember to say Bismillah before we eat."

"Bismillah," they all said together. After finishing her meal, Fatima said, "Alhamdulillah," which means "Praise be to Allah."

After dinner, Fatima and Ali sat with their Jaddi, who started to tell them about good manners. "Adab," Jaddi said, "means good manners and proper behavior. In Islam, we are taught to always be kind, respectful, and helpful to others. This makes Allah happy and makes our hearts feel good too."

Fatima nodded, remembering how she had helped Mr. Hasan and Jaddati earlier. She felt proud and happy to have shown good adab.

Before leaving, Fatima's Jaddati handed her a small gift. "This is for you, Fatima, for being such a wonderful helper today."

Fatima thanked her Jaddati and said, "Alhamdulillah," feeling grateful.

That night, when Fatima was back home and getting ready for bed, she said, "Bismillah," and thanked Allah for teaching her the importance of good manners. She knew she wanted to continue showing good adab every day.

Moral of the Story: Always be kind, respectful, and helpful to others. This is the best way to show good manners or adab.

Chapter 24

The Story of the Kaaba: The Sacred House

Fatima lived in a small village with her family. She loved learning about her faith, Islam. One day, her Ummi called her and said, "Fatima, today we will learn about the Kaaba, the Sacred House."

Fatima's eyes sparkled with curiosity. "What is the Kaaba, Ummi?" she asked. Ummi smiled and said, "The Kaaba is a very special place in Islam. It is in the city of Mecca, and all Muslims face it when they pray." Fatima's little brother, Ali, joined them. "Assalamu Alaikum, Akhi," Fatima greeted him. "Wa Alaikum Assalam, Ukhti," Ali replied. He also wanted to hear about the Kaaba.

Ummi began to explain. "A long time ago, Prophet Ibrahim (peace be upon him) and his son Ismail (peace be upon him) built the Kaaba. They built it to worship Allah. It is a simple, cube-shaped building."

Fatima was amazed. "Bismillah, that's so interesting! Why do we face the Kaaba when we pray?" "Facing the Kaaba when we pray helps us stay united," Ummi explained. "No matter where we are in the world, we all face the same direction. This shows that we are one big family in Islam."

Fatima and Ali nodded. They wanted to know more. "Can we visit the Kaaba?" Ali asked.

"Yes, Akhi," Ummi said. "Many Muslims visit the Kaaba during Hajj or Umrah. These are special trips to Mecca. When people reach the Kaaba, they walk around it seven times. This is called Tawaf."

Fatima imagined people from all over the world coming together. "What do they say when they walk around the Kaaba?" "They say 'Labbaik Allahumma Labbaik,' which means 'Here I am, O Allah, here I am,'" Ummi replied. "It is a way to show their love and obedience to Allah."

That evening, Fatima's Abu joined them. "Assalamu Alaikum, Abu!" Fatima and Ali said together. "Wa Alaikum Assalam, my dear children," Abu replied, hugging them. Ummi told Abu about their conversation. Abu added, "Did you know the Kaaba is covered with a special cloth called the Kiswa? It is black and has beautiful golden writing on it."

"Wow, Alhamdulillah, that's beautiful!" Fatima said. Abu continued, "The Kaaba is also where we find the Black Stone, called Al-Hajar Al-Aswad. It is placed in one corner of the Kaaba. When Muslims walk around the Kaaba, they try to touch or kiss the Black Stone if they can."

Fatima and Ali listened carefully. They felt excited about learning so much about the Kaaba.

The next day, their Jaddi came to visit. He was happy to hear about their interest in the Kaaba. Fatima asked, "Jaddi, why is the Kaaba so important to us?" Jaddi smiled and said, "The Kaaba is important because it is the first house built for the worship of Allah. It reminds us to always pray and be good Muslims. It is a symbol of our faith and unity."

Fatima felt proud to be a Muslim. She wanted to learn more about her religion and visit the Kaaba one day.

That night, before going to bed, Fatima said, "Bismillah" and thanked Allah for teaching her about the Kaaba. She knew that being a good Muslim meant having faith and showing love to Allah.

Moral of the Story: The Kaaba is a special place for all Muslims. It teaches us about faith, unity, and the importance of worshipping Allah.

Chapter 25

Understanding Jumu'ah: The Friday Prayer

Fatima loved Fridays because they were special in her family. Every Friday was Jumu'ah, the day of the Friday Prayer. When she woke up, she said, "Bismillah," and ran to the garden where her Abu was tending to the plants.

"Assalamu Alaikum, Abu," Fatima greeted him.

"Wa Alaikum Assalam, Fatima," Abu replied with a warm smile. "Are you excited for Jumu'ah today?"

"Yes, Abu! I can't wait to go to the mosque with you and Akhi," Fatima said eagerly.

After breakfast, Fatima and her little brother, Ali, helped their Ummi prepare for the day. They tidied up the house and put on their best clothes. Fatima wore a lovely dress, and Ali wore his favorite shirt. They both looked very nice.

"Assalamu Alaikum, Ummi!" they both said when they saw their mother.

"Wa Alaikum Assalam, my dear children," Ummi replied. "You both look wonderful. Today is a special day."

Fatima and Ali were curious about why Jumu'ah was so special. "Ummi, can you tell us why Jumu'ah is important?" Ali asked.

Ummi smiled and said, "Jumu'ah is the most important day of the week for Muslims. On this day, we gather at the mosque for a special prayer. It is a time to remember Allah and be with our community."

Before they left for the mosque, Abu gathered the family and said, "Let's say 'Bismillah' before we go."

"Bismillah," they all said together. The family walked to the mosque, greeting their friends and neighbors along the way. Everyone was dressed nicely and greeted each other with "Assalamu Alaikum." The mosque looked beautiful and peaceful.

Inside the mosque, Fatima and Ali sat with their parents. The Imam began the Khutbah, talking about being kind, helping others, and remembering Allah. Fatima listened carefully, trying to understand the important lessons.

After the Khutbah, everyone stood up to pray together. Fatima loved how everyone moved in unison, bowing and prostrating together. It made her feel connected to her family and her community. She whispered, "Alhamdulillah," feeling grateful to be part of such a special gathering.

When the prayer was over, the family returned home. Ummi prepared a special lunch, and they all sat together to eat. They shared stories and laughed, enjoying their time together. Fatima felt very happy and thankful for the day.

In the afternoon, Fatima and her family decided to visit the local orphanage. They brought gifts and sweets for the children there. "Assalamu Alaikum, everyone!" Fatima greeted the children.

"Wa Alaikum Assalam," the children replied with big smiles.

Fatima and Ali played games with the children and shared their toys. They felt happy seeing the children smile and laugh. Fatima's Abu explained, "Jumu'ah is not just about prayer; it is also about doing good deeds and helping others."

Fatima nodded, understanding that Jumu'ah was a day of giving and kindness. Before they left, Fatima hugged one of the little girls and said, "Alhamdulillah for such a wonderful day."

That night, before going to bed, Fatima said, "Bismillah" and thanked Allah for the wonderful Jumu'ah. She knew that every Friday, she would look forward to this special day.

Moral of the Story: Jumu'ah, the Friday Prayer, is a special time for Muslims to come together, pray, and remember Allah. It also teaches us the importance of doing good deeds and helping others.

Chapter 26

The Story of Islamic Months: The Hijri Calendar

In a small village, there lived a family who loved to learn about the world. The family had a kind Ummi and Abu, a playful Akhi named Ahmed, and a curious Ukhti named Aisha. They also had a wise Jaddi and a loving Jaddati.

One sunny morning, Ummi gathered everyone in the living room. "Bismillah," she began, "Today, we will learn about the Islamic months and the Hijri calendar." Ahmed and Aisha were very excited. "The Hijri calendar," explained Abu, "is a special calendar used by Muslims all around the world. It started when our Prophet Muhammad (peace be upon him) moved from Makkah to Madinah. This journey is called the Hijra."

Aisha raised her hand, "How many months are there in the Hijri calendar, Ummi?" "There are twelve months," Ummi replied with a smile. "Each month has a special meaning and many have important events. Let's start with the first month, Muharram."

"Muharram is a very special month," Jaddi added. "It's the month of Allah. The Day of Ashura is in Muharram, a day when many people fast and remember important events in our history."

The family nodded, and Abu continued, "The second month is Safar. Some people believe it's a month of hardships, but we trust in Allah and say 'Alhamdulillah' for everything we have."

Aisha looked curious. "What comes next, Baba?"

"The third month is Rabi' al-Awwal," Abu replied. "This month is very special because our beloved Prophet Muhammad (peace be upon him) was born in Rabi' al-Awwal." "And then comes Rabi' al-Thani," Ummi said. "It is a continuation of the blessings of Rabi' al-Awwal." Ahmed clapped his hands. "What about the next months, Abu?"

"The fifth month is Jumada al-Awwal, and the sixth is Jumada al-Thani," Abu explained. "These months remind us of the changing seasons and the blessings of Allah."

"Rajab is the seventh month," Jaddi said softly. "It is a sacred month, one of the four sacred months in Islam."

"The eighth month is Sha'ban," Jaddati added. "During Sha'ban, we prepare for the holy month of Ramadan. Many people fast and pray more in Sha'ban."

Aisha and Ahmed's eyes sparkled. "Ramadan is my favorite!" Aisha exclaimed.

"Yes, Ramadan is the ninth month," Ummi said with a warm smile. "It is the month of fasting, prayer, and Quran. It is a very blessed time for all Muslims."

"The tenth month is Shawwal," Abu continued. "After fasting for a whole month, we celebrate Eid al-Fitr in Shawwal. It's a time of joy and gratitude."

"The eleventh month is Dhu al-Qa'dah," Jaddati said. "It is another sacred month, a time of peace and preparation for the Hajj pilgrimage."

"And finally, the twelfth month is Dhu al-Hijjah," Abu concluded. "It is the month of Hajj, when Muslims from all over the world go to Makkah to perform the pilgrimage. Eid al-Adha is also celebrated in this month."

The children were fascinated. "Shukran, Ummi and Abu," Ahmed said. "We learned so much today!" "Alhamdulillah," said Ummi. "Always remember, every month is special and has its own blessings."

Moral of the Story: Every month in the Hijri calendar is important and teaches us to be thankful and to remember Allah.

Chapter 27

The Night of Power: Laylat al-Qadr

During the holy month of Ramadan, Ahmed and Aisha were very excited. They loved Ramadan because it was a time for fasting, prayer, and family. One evening, while they were having iftar, their Ummi said, "Bismillah, today we will learn about a very special night called Laylat al-Qadr, the Night of Power."

Aisha looked curious. "What is Laylat al-Qadr, Ummi?"

Ummi smiled and replied, "Laylat al-Qadr is the most special night of the year. It is a night in Ramadan when the Quran was first sent down from Allah to Prophet Muhammad (peace be upon him). It is a night full of blessings and mercy."

Abu added, "Laylat al-Qadr is mentioned in the Quran. Allah says that this night is better than a thousand months. Imagine how many blessings we can get in just one night!"

Ahmed's eyes widened. "Wow, Baba! What should we do on this special night?"

Abu replied, "We should pray, read the Quran, and ask Allah for forgiveness. It is a night to make lots of du'a and to be close to Allah."

Jaddi, who was sitting nearby, said, "Alhamdulillah, it is also a time to remember those who need our help. We should be kind and generous."

Aisha asked, "When does Laylat al-Qadr happen, Jaddi?"

Jaddi explained, "Laylat al-Qadr happens in the last ten nights of Ramadan. Many people believe it is on one of the odd-numbered nights, like the 21st, 23rd, 25th, 27th, or 29th night. But we should try to pray and do good deeds on all of the last ten nights to make sure we don't miss it."

Jaddati, with a gentle smile, said, "On Laylat al-Qadr, the angels come down to the earth, bringing peace and blessings. It is a very peaceful night."

Ahmed looked thoughtful. "How can we make sure we get the blessings of Laylat al-Qadr, Yumma?"

Ummi replied, "We should stay awake and pray, read the Quran, and be kind to everyone. Remember to make du'a for yourself, your family, and all the people in the world. Always start with Bismillah and end with Alhamdulillah."

Aisha and Ahmed nodded, feeling excited to experience Laylat al-Qadr. They decided to prepare by learning more du'as and helping Ummi and Abu with iftar and suhoor.

One night, as they gathered for iftar, Ummi said, "Tonight might be Laylat al-Qadr. Let's pray together and ask Allah for all the good things we want."

After iftar, the family prayed together. Ahmed and Aisha felt a special peace in their hearts. They read from the Quran, made du'a, and thanked Allah for all the blessings they had.

As the night went on, they felt closer to Allah and to each other. They knew that Laylat al-Qadr was a gift, a chance to become better and to ask for Allah's mercy and guidance.

In the morning, Ahmed and Aisha felt very happy. They had spent the night in prayer and good deeds. They felt the special blessings of Laylat al-Qadr and knew that Allah had heard their prayers.

Moral of the Story: Laylat al-Qadr is a very special night full of blessings and mercy. It teaches us to pray, be kind, and ask Allah for all the good things we need.

Chapter 28

The Meaning of Bismillah: In the Name of Allah

Ali loved to learn new things every day. One morning, as he got ready for school, his Ummi said, "Ali, today we will learn about the importance of saying 'Bismillah.'" Ali was curious and asked, "Why is it so important, Ummi?"

Ummi smiled and explained, "Bismillah means 'In the name of Allah.' When we say Bismillah, we are asking Allah to bless what we are about to do. It helps us remember Allah and do things in a good way."

Ali thought about this as he put on his shoes. He said, "Bismillah," and felt happy to start his day with Allah's blessings. As they walked to school, Abu joined them and said, "Ali, do you know that saying Bismillah can help you in many ways?"

Ali looked up at his Abu and asked, "How, Abu?"

Abu explained, "When we say Bismillah before eating, it reminds us to be thankful for the food we have. It also makes the food a blessing for us. Let's say Bismillah together before we eat lunch today."

At school, Ali's teacher, Mr. Ahmed, talked about how saying Bismillah can help us focus and do our best. "When you start your work with Bismillah, you are asking Allah to help you," Mr. Ahmed said. Ali said, "Bismillah," before starting his drawing and felt proud of his work.

Later, during recess, Ali saw his friend Sara struggling to climb the jungle gym. He remembered what his Abu said and told Sara, "Say Bismillah before you try again." Sara nodded, said "Bismillah," and tried again. This time, she made it to the top! "Thank you, Ali," Sara said with a big smile.

After school, Ali's Jaddi came to visit. He brought some fruits from his garden. "Ali, do you know that the Prophet Muhammad always said Bismillah before starting anything?" Jaddi said. "It's a way to ask Allah to make everything we do successful."

They sat down to eat the fruits, and Jaddati joined them. She reminded Ali, "When you say Bismillah before drinking water, it helps you remember Allah and be grateful for even the simple things in life." Ali said, "Bismillah," before drinking his water and felt thankful.

In the evening, Ali's Ukhti, Fatima, showed him how to say Bismillah before starting her homework. "It helps me concentrate and do my best," she said. Ali decided to do the same with his homework and found it easier to focus.

Before bed, Baba told Ali a bedtime story. "Do you know, Ali, that saying Bismillah can protect us?" Baba said. "When you start your day, your meals, your work, or even play with Bismillah, you are asking Allah to keep you safe and help you."

Ali lay in bed, thinking about all the ways saying Bismillah had helped him and his family that day. He felt peaceful and happy. He said, "Alhamdulillah," thanking Allah for teaching him this beautiful way to start everything.

As Ali drifted off to sleep, he dreamed of a world where everyone remembered to say Bismillah, making their actions blessed and guided by Allah's love and protection.

Moral of the Story: Saying "Bismillah" helps us remember Allah and makes our actions blessed, guiding us to do things in the best way.

Chapter 29

The Big Family of the Ummah

In a small village, there was a boy named Ali. Ali lived with his Ummi, Baba, and little sister, Ikht. Every morning, Ali would wake up and say, "Bismillah," which means "In the name of Allah," before he started his day. He loved his family very much.

One sunny day, Ali's Ummi told him, "Today, we are going to visit Jaddi and Jaddati." Ali was excited. He loved spending time with his grandfather and grandmother. They lived in a house not too far from theirs. Before they left, Ali's Baba said, "Alhamdulillah, we are lucky to have such a big family."

As they walked, Ali saw many other families. He saw Akhi playing with his friends, and he waved at them. They greeted each other with "As-salamu alaykum," which means "peace be upon you." Ali felt happy to be part of such a friendly community.

When they arrived at Jaddi and Jaddati's house, Jaddi was sitting under a big tree. He smiled and said, "Marhaba, Ali!" which means "Hello." Jaddati came out of the house with a big smile and hugged Ali tightly. "It's so good to see you, dear," she said.

After lunch, Jaddi gathered all the children around him. "Do you know what Ummah means?" he asked. Ali and the other children shook their heads. Jaddi smiled and began to explain. "Ummah means the global Muslim community. It's like a big family that includes all Muslims around the world."

Ali listened carefully. Jaddi continued, "When we say 'As-salamu alaykum' to someone, we are wishing them peace. We are showing that we care about them, just like we care about our own family."

Ali thought about this. He remembered how Akhi and his friends had greeted him warmly. He realized that they were all part of the Ummah.

Later, Ali and Ikht helped Jaddati in the garden. As they worked, Jaddati said, "In our Ummah, we help each other. Just like you are helping me now, we should always try to help others."

Ali nodded. He enjoyed helping his Jaddati. He thought about how he could help more people in his village. Maybe he could help his friends with their homework or share his toys with children who didn't have any.

As the day ended, Ali and his family said goodbye to Jaddi and Jaddati. They hugged them and said, "Ma'a as-salama," which means "goodbye." On the way home, Ali's Baba said, "We are very lucky to be part of the Ummah. Remember to always be kind and helpful to everyone."

That night, as Ali went to bed, he said, "Alhamdulillah," thanking Allah for his big family and the Ummah. He knew that being part of the Ummah meant he was never alone. There were always people who cared about him and whom he could care for too.

Ali dreamed of a world where everyone was kind and helpful, just like in his village. He knew that if everyone followed the teachings of the Ummah, the world would be a better place.

Moral of the Story: Always be kind and helpful to everyone, because we are all part of one big family called the Ummah.

Chapter 30

Learning About Islamic Celebrations

Ali was a curious boy who loved to learn new things. One day, his Ummi told him, "Ali, today we will learn about our Islamic celebrations." Ali was excited and said, "Bismillah," ready to start his day.

First, Ummi talked about Ramadan. "Ramadan is a special month," she said. "We fast from sunrise to sunset. This means we don't eat or drink during the day. It helps us remember to be grateful for what we have and to think about those who are less fortunate." Ali listened carefully. He remembered how last year he tried fasting for a day and how proud everyone was of him.

Then, Ummi explained about Eid al-Fitr. "At the end of Ramadan, we have a big celebration called Eid al-Fitr. On this day, we wear new clothes, pray together, and visit our family and friends. We say, 'Eid Mubarak!' which means 'Blessed Eid.' We also give gifts and eat delicious food." Ali smiled, thinking about the fun he had last Eid with his cousins and the sweets Jaddati made.

Later that day, Baba came home and greeted Ali with "As-salamu alaykum." He sat down with Ali and Ummi and continued the lesson. "There is another important celebration called Eid al-Adha," Baba said. "This Eid comes after the Hajj, the pilgrimage to Mecca. On Eid al-Adha, we remember the story of Prophet Ibrahim and his devotion to Allah. We also share meat with family, friends, and those in need."

Ali was fascinated. "Baba, I remember we gave meat to our neighbors last year," he said. Baba nodded and said, "Yes, Ali. It is important to share and help others, just like Prophet Ibrahim did."

In the evening, Jaddi and Jaddati came to visit. They brought some sweets and sat with Ali. "Let's talk about Mawlid al-Nabi," Jaddi said. "This is the celebration of the Prophet Muhammad's birthday. We remember his teachings and how he showed us to be kind and honest. Many people sing songs, read stories about his life, and give food to the poor."

Jaddati added, "On this day, we also say, 'Salam' to each other and pray for peace. It is a day to remember the love and mercy of the Prophet."

Ali loved hearing these stories. He realized how each celebration was special and taught important lessons about kindness, sharing, and gratitude.

Before bed, Ali's Ukhti, Fatima, came to his room. "What did you learn today, Khuya?" she asked. Ali told her all about Ramadan, Eid al-Fitr, Eid al-Adha, and Mawlid al-Nabi. Fatima smiled and said, "You learned a lot today, Ali. Alhamdulillah, we are blessed with such wonderful traditions."

The next day, Ummi told Ali about another celebration called Isra and Mi'raj. "This is the night journey and ascension of Prophet Muhammad. It's a special night when we remember the Prophet's journey from Mecca to Jerusalem and then to the heavens. We pray extra prayers and remember his teachings."

Baba also mentioned Ashura. "Ashura is an important day in the month of Muharram. We remember the great sacrifices made by Prophet Muhammad's grandson, Imam Hussein. It teaches us about standing up for what is right and being brave."

As Ali lay in bed, he thought about all the celebrations. He felt happy to be part of such a rich and caring community. He said, "Alhamdulillah," thanking Allah for his family and the beautiful celebrations they enjoyed together.

Moral of the Story: Celebrations are special times to remember important lessons, share with others, and be grateful for our blessings.

Chapter 31

Understanding the Sunnah: Following the Prophet's Way

Ali loved learning new things, especially about how to be a good person. One day, his Abu said, "Ali, today we will learn about the Sunnah, the practices of Prophet Muhammad." Ali was excited to start his day.

Abu began, "The Sunnah is the way Prophet Muhammad lived his life. By following his actions and teachings, we can learn to be kind, honest, and helpful." Ali listened carefully, wanting to know more.

First, Abu told Ali about how the Prophet always started his day by thanking Allah for a new day. "He would say, 'Alhamdulillah,' which means 'All praise is due to Allah,'" Abu explained. "This helps us remember to be grateful for all the blessings we have." Ali decided to try this every morning.

Next, Abu showed Ali how the Prophet would always greet others with a smile and say, "As-salamu alaykum," which means "peace be upon you." "A smile is a simple way to show kindness," Abu said. Ali practiced smiling and saying, "As-salamu alaykum" to his family.

Later, Ali's Ummi joined them. "The Prophet Muhammad always took care of his family," she said. "He would help with chores and be gentle and kind to everyone." Ummi showed Ali how to help set the table for dinner. "Helping each other makes our home a happy place," she said.

In the afternoon, Ali's Jaddi came to visit. He told Ali about how the Prophet loved to spend time in nature. "He appreciated the beauty of Allah's creation," Jaddi said. "Let's go for a walk and admire the trees and flowers." Ali and Jaddi went for a walk, and Ali noticed the birds singing and the flowers blooming. "It's beautiful, Jaddi," Ali said. Jaddi smiled and said, "Remember to thank Allah for all this beauty."

In the evening, Ali's Ukhti, Fatima, showed him how the Prophet Muhammad would share his food with others. "He always made sure that no one around him was hungry," she said. They prepared some food together and took it to a neighbor who wasn't feeling well. The neighbor smiled and said, "Jazak Allahu Khairan," which means "May Allah reward you with goodness." Ali felt happy to help.

Before bed, Ali's Baba told him about the importance of honesty. "The Prophet Muhammad was known as Al-Amin, which means 'the trustworthy,'" Baba said. "He always told the truth and kept his promises." Baba explained that being honest helps people trust each other. Ali promised to always tell the truth.

Ali also learned that the Prophet Muhammad prayed five times a day. "Prayer helps us stay close to Allah," his Abu said. They prayed together, and Ali felt peaceful.

As Ali lay in bed, he thought about all the things he had learned. He felt proud to follow the Sunnah and be more like Prophet Muhammad. He said, "Alhamdulillah," thanking Allah for his family and the lessons they had taught him.

Ali dreamed of being kind, honest, and helpful, just like the Prophet. He knew that by following the Sunnah, he could make the world a better place.

Moral of the Story: Following the Sunnah teaches us to be kind, honest, and helpful, making our world a better and more peaceful place.

Chapter 32

The Role of the Mufti: Islamic Scholar

Ali loved learning about different people in his community. One day, his Abu said, "Ali, today we will learn about the mufti, an important Islamic scholar." Ali was excited and said, "Bismillah," ready to start his day.

Abu explained, "A mufti is a person who has studied the Quran and the teachings of Prophet Muhammad. They help people by giving them advice based on Islamic teachings." Ali listened carefully, eager to know more.

Later, Abu took Ali to visit the local mosque. There, they met Mufti Ibrahim. Mufti Ibrahim greeted them with a warm smile and said, "As-salamu alaykum." Ali replied, "Wa alaykum as-salam," feeling happy to meet him.

Mufti Ibrahim invited them to sit and have some tea. As they sipped their tea, Mufti Ibrahim began to explain his role. "I help people understand what Islam teaches us," he said. "If someone has a question about how to pray, how to be kind, or what to do in a difficult situation, they can come to me for guidance."

Ali thought this was very interesting. He asked, "How do you know all the answers, Mufti Ibrahim?" The mufti smiled and said, "I have studied for many years, reading the Quran and learning from other scholars. I also pray to Allah to help me give the best advice."

Ummi joined them and said, "Mufti Ibrahim, can you tell Ali about how you help the community?" Mufti Ibrahim nodded and shared a story. "One day, a man came to me very worried. He did not know how to help his friend who was sad. I told him that the Prophet Muhammad taught us to be kind and supportive. I suggested he spend time with his friend and remind him that Allah is always there for us. The man followed my advice, and his friend felt much better."

Ali was amazed. "So you help people feel better and understand what to do?" he asked. Mufti Ibrahim nodded, "Yes, Ali. It is important to help each other and follow the teachings of Islam."

In the afternoon, Ali's Jaddi came to visit. He asked Mufti Ibrahim about how to teach children to be good Muslims. The mufti said, "Teach them by showing them good examples. Pray together, read stories from the Quran, and talk about the Prophet's kindness. Children learn a lot by watching and listening."

Jaddati then asked, "Mufti Ibrahim, how can we help our neighbors who are not Muslims?" Mufti Ibrahim smiled and said, "The Prophet Muhammad taught us to be kind to everyone, no matter their religion.

Help them when they need it, be friendly, and show respect. This is how we can live in peace together."

In the evening, Ali's Ukhti, Fatima, asked, "Mufti Ibrahim, what should I do if I make a mistake?" The mufti replied, "We all make mistakes, Fatima. The important thing is to say sorry and try to do better next time. Pray to Allah for forgiveness and learn from your mistakes."

As they walked home, Ali thought about all the things he had learned. He felt grateful to have met Mufti Ibrahim and understood the important role of a mufti in the community. He said, "Alhamdulillah," thanking Allah for such knowledgeable and kind people.

Ali dreamed of helping others just like Mufti Ibrahim. He knew that by following the guidance of a mufti, he could be a better person and help make the world a kinder place.

Moral of the Story: A mufti helps us understand how to live kindly and follow Islamic teachings, making our community a better place.

Chapter 33

The Story of the Mihrab: The Prayer Niche

Ali loved going to the mosque with his Abu. One day, as they walked to the mosque, his Abu said, "Ali, today I will tell you about something very special in the mosque called the mihrab." Ali was curious and said, "Bismillah," ready to learn.

When they arrived at the mosque, Ali saw many people getting ready to pray. Abu pointed to a beautiful, decorated niche in the wall. "That is the mihrab," he said. "It shows us the direction of the Kaaba in Mecca, which is the direction we face when we pray."

Ali looked closely at the mihrab. It was carved with beautiful patterns and Arabic words. "Why is it so important, Abu?" he asked.

Abu smiled and explained, "The mihrab helps us face the right way during our prayers. It reminds us that all Muslims around the world are united in their prayer, facing the same direction."

Ali's Ummi joined them and said, "Ali, do you know that the mihrab also helps the Imam? The Imam stands in front of the mihrab to lead the prayers. This way, everyone can follow him and pray together." Ali nodded, thinking about how the mihrab helped everyone stay together in their worship.

Later, Ali's Jaddi came to the mosque and told him more about the mihrab. "In the old days," Jaddi said, "people didn't have clocks to tell the prayer times. They would look at the sky or listen for the call to prayer. The mihrab was a special place that helped them know where to stand and pray."

Ali was fascinated. "So the mihrab has been helping people for a long time?" he asked. Jaddi nodded, "Yes, Ali. It has always been an important part of the mosque."

Jaddati added, "The mihrab is also a reminder of the Prophet Muhammad's mosque in Medina. It was simple but very special, just like our mihrab." Ali imagined the Prophet's mosque and felt proud to be part of this tradition.

Ali's Akhi, Ahmed, joined them and said, "The mihrab is often decorated with beautiful designs to honor its importance. It's not just a simple niche; it's a work of art that shows our love for Allah." Ali looked at the intricate patterns and felt inspired by their beauty.

In the evening, Ali's Ukhti, Fatima, asked him what he had learned. Ali told her about the mihrab and how it shows the direction of Mecca. Fatima said, "That's amazing, Khuya. The mihrab helps us feel connected to all Muslims around the world."

Before bed, Baba told Ali a story about when he was a boy. "I remember my first time seeing the mihrab," Baba said. "I was just as curious as you. It made me feel like I was part of something big and important." Ali listened carefully, feeling the same sense of belonging.

Baba continued, "The mihrab is also a place of focus. When we stand before it, we are reminded to clear our minds and concentrate on our prayers. It helps us connect with Allah in a special way." Ali understood how important it was to focus during prayer.

As Ali lay in bed, he thought about the mihrab and its significance. He felt grateful to have learned about it and said, "Alhamdulillah," thanking Allah for the knowledge.

Moral of the Story: The mihrab helps us face the right direction in prayer, reminding us that all Muslims are united in their worship of Allah.

Chapter 34

Understanding Dhikr: Remembrance of Allah

Ali loved spending time with his family and learning new things about his faith. One day, his Abu said, "Ali, today we will learn about the practice of dhikr, which means remembering Allah." Ali was curious and said, "Bismillah," ready to learn.

Abu explained, "Dhikr is when we say special words to remember Allah. We say 'SubhanAllah,' which means 'Glory be to Allah,' 'Alhamdulillah,' which means 'All praise is due to Allah,' and 'Allahu Akbar,' which means 'Allah is the Greatest.' These words help us feel close to Allah."

Ali thought about this as he helped his Ummi in the garden. They planted flowers together, and Ummi said, "Ali, let's say 'SubhanAllah' when we see the beauty of these flowers." Ali looked at the colorful blooms and said, "SubhanAllah," feeling grateful for the beauty around him.

Later, Ali's Jaddi came to visit. He brought some delicious fruits from his garden. "Ali, do you know that saying 'Alhamdulillah' is a way to thank Allah for the good things we have?" Jaddi said. "Let's say 'Alhamdulillah' for these tasty fruits." Ali took a bite and said, "Alhamdulillah," enjoying the sweet taste.

In the afternoon, Ali's Akhi, Ahmed, showed him how to use a small string of beads called a tasbih. "We use this to help count our dhikr," Ahmed explained. "You can say 'SubhanAllah,' 'Alhamdulillah,' and 'Allahu Akbar' as you move your fingers over each bead." Ali tried it and found it calming. He liked the feeling of the beads in his hand and the peaceful rhythm of the words.

As the sun began to set, Ali and his family gathered for Maghrib prayer. After praying, Ali's Ukhti, Fatima, said, "Dhikr can also be done after our prayers to help us stay close to Allah." They all said, "SubhanAllah," "Alhamdulillah," and "Allahu Akbar" together, feeling peaceful and connected. Ali noticed how the words made him feel calm and centered.

In the evening, Jaddati told Ali a story about the Prophet Muhammad. "The Prophet loved to do dhikr and taught us its importance," she said. "He said that remembering Allah fills our hearts with peace and keeps us strong in our faith." Ali listened carefully, feeling inspired to do more dhikr. Jaddati added, "Even when the Prophet faced challenges, he would remember Allah and find strength."

Before bed, Baba sat with Ali and said, "Ali, do you know that dhikr can also help us when we feel scared or worried? Saying 'Allahu

Akbar' reminds us that Allah is the greatest and can help us through anything." Ali nodded, remembering a time when he felt afraid and saying dhikr made him feel better. Baba shared a story from his own childhood about how dhikr helped him stay calm during a storm.

Ali's Ummi then came in and said, "Ali, remember to say 'Bismillah' before you start anything and 'Alhamdulillah' when you finish. It's a way to include Allah in everything you do." Ali thought about this and promised to remember.

As Ali lay in bed, he thought about all the ways dhikr had helped him that day. He felt grateful for the reminders to remember Allah in everything he did. He said, "Alhamdulillah," thanking Allah for the peace and happiness he felt. He also whispered, "SubhanAllah" for the beautiful day and "Allahu Akbar" for the strength he felt in his heart.

Moral of the Story: Dhikr, or remembering Allah, helps us feel close to Allah, brings peace to our hearts, and keeps us strong in our faith.

Chapter 35

The Story of Iman: Faith in Islam

Ali loved learning new things about his faith. One day, his Abu said, "Ali, today we will talk about iman, which means faith in Allah." Ali was curious and said, "Bismillah," ready to learn.

Abu began, "Iman is believing in Allah, His angels, His books, His messengers, the Day of Judgment, and that everything happens by Allah's will. It's very important in a Muslim's life because it helps us stay close to Allah and be good people."

Ali thought about this as he helped his Ummi in the kitchen. They were making a delicious cake. Ummi said, "Ali, just like we need all the ingredients to make this cake, we need iman to live a good life. It gives us strength and guidance." Ali nodded, understanding how important iman was.

Later, Ali's Jaddi came to visit. He sat with Ali and said, "Iman helps us trust Allah even when things are hard. Do you remember when you were scared of the dark? Saying a prayer and trusting Allah made you feel safe." Ali remembered and felt thankful for his iman.

In the afternoon, Ali's Akhi, Ahmed, took him to the park. They saw a tree with strong roots. Ahmed said, "Iman is like the roots of this tree. It keeps us strong and helps us stand tall, no matter what happens." Ali looked at the tree and felt proud to have strong iman.

As the sun began to set, Ali and his family gathered for Maghrib prayer. After praying, Ali's Ukhti, Fatima, said, "Iman also helps us be kind and honest. When we have faith in Allah, we want to do good things and help others." Fatima then told Ali about how she helped a friend at school. "Today, a new girl was feeling lonely and shy, so I invited her to play with me and my friends. It made her very happy."

Ali smiled and said, "That was a very kind thing to do, Ukhti. Iman helped you be a good friend."

In the evening, Jaddati told Ali a story about the Prophet Muhammad. "The Prophet had strong iman and always trusted Allah, even in difficult times. His faith helped him be brave and kind." Ali listened carefully, feeling inspired to have strong iman like the Prophet.

Before bed, Baba sat with Ali and said, "Ali, do you know that iman also helps us when we feel sad or worried? Trusting Allah can make us feel better because we know He is always with us." Ali nodded, remembering a time when he felt sad and praying made him feel better.

Ali's Ummi then came in and said, "Ali, remember to say 'Alhamdulillah' for all the good things in your life. Being thankful is part of having strong iman." Ali thought about all the things he was thankful for and said, "Alhamdulillah."

As Ali lay in bed, he thought about all the ways iman had helped him that day. He felt grateful for his faith and said, "Alhamdulillah," thanking Allah for the strength and guidance iman gave him. He also whispered, "Bismillah" for the new day to come and the opportunities to strengthen his faith.

Ali drifted off to sleep, dreaming of a world where everyone had strong iman, filling their hearts with trust in Allah and making the world a better place. He felt a deep connection to his family and his faith, knowing that iman was a special gift that brought them all closer to Allah.

He felt a deep connection to his family and his faith, knowing that iman was a special gift that brought them all closer to Allah.

Moral of the Story: Iman, or faith in Allah, helps us stay strong, be good people, and trust Allah in all situations.

Chapter 36

The Importance of Cleanliness in Islam

Ali loved to play outside, but he sometimes got very dirty. One day, his Ummi said, "Ali, today we will learn about the importance of cleanliness in Islam." Ali was curious and said, "Bismillah," ready to learn. Ummi explained, "Cleanliness is very important in Islam. It is part of our faith. We must keep our bodies, clothes, and surroundings clean." Ali listened carefully as Ummi continued, "Before we pray, we do wudu, which is washing our hands, face, and feet. This helps us stay clean and ready to talk to Allah."

Ali thought about this as he helped his Abu wash the dishes. Abu said, "Ali, saying 'Bismillah' before we start helps us remember that we are doing a good deed. Keeping our kitchen clean means we can prepare food that is healthy and good for us." Ali enjoyed helping and felt proud to be clean.

Later, Ali's Jaddi came to visit. He sat with Ali and said, "Cleanliness is not just about our bodies, but also our hearts. When we say 'Alhamdulillah,' we are cleaning our hearts by being thankful to Allah." Ali smiled, understanding that being clean inside was just as important as being clean outside.

In the afternoon, Ali's Akhi, Ahmed, showed him how to clean his toys. "If we keep our toys clean, they last longer and are more fun to play with," Ahmed said. Ali enjoyed washing his toys and felt happy knowing they were clean.

As the sun began to set, Ali and his family gathered for Maghrib prayer. Before praying, they all did wudu. Ali's Ukhti, Fatima, said, "See how refreshing it feels to be clean before we pray? It helps us focus and feel close to Allah." Ali nodded, feeling the cool water on his skin and the peace in his heart.

After prayers, Ali's Jaddi shared a story about the Prophet Muhammad. "The Prophet always kept himself and his home clean. He said that cleanliness is half of faith. He would wash his hands before and after eating and kept his clothes and body clean." Ali felt inspired to follow the Prophet's example.

In the evening, Ali's family decided to have a special clean-up day. They all worked together to tidy the house and garden. Ali's Jaddati explained, "Keeping our home clean is part of taking care of the blessings Allah has given us." Ali enjoyed working with his family and seeing the house sparkle.

Before bed, Baba sat with Ali and said, "Ali, do you know that keeping our environment clean is also important? If we see trash on the ground, we should pick it up and throw it away properly. This helps keep our world beautiful and healthy." Ali remembered picking up trash in the park with his family and felt proud of his good deeds.

Ali's Ummi then came in and said, "Ali, remember to brush your teeth and wash your hands before bed. This keeps you healthy and ready for a good night's sleep." Ali brushed his teeth, washed his hands, and said, "Alhamdulillah," for all the lessons he learned about cleanliness.

As Ali lay in bed, he thought about all the ways he could stay clean and help others do the same. He felt thankful for his faith and the guidance it provided. He whispered, "Bismillah," excited for the new day and the chance to practice cleanliness.

The next morning, at school, Ali saw some of his classmates leaving their trash on the ground. He kindly reminded them, "We should always keep our surroundings clean. It's important to pick up after ourselves." His friends agreed and helped clean up the playground. Ali felt proud to be practicing what he had learned. He realized that cleanliness was not just about keeping his own body and home clean but also about caring for the environment and helping others understand its importance.

Moral of the Story: Cleanliness is very important in Islam. It helps us stay healthy, feel good, and be close to Allah.

Chapter 37

The Story of Islamic Greetings: Salam

In a small, happy village, there lived a little boy named Ahmed. Ahmed was kind and always liked to make people smile. He lived with his Ummi, Abu, and his baby sister, Ikht Aisha. Ahmed also had a Jaddi and Jaddati who lived nearby. Every morning, Ahmed would greet his family and friends with a big smile.

One sunny day, Ahmed woke up early and said, **"Bismillah,"** before starting his day. He rushed to the living room where his Ummi was watering the plants. **"Assalamu Alaikum, Ummi!"** Ahmed greeted her. This greeting means "Peace be upon you," and it is used to wish someone peace and safety. Ummi smiled and replied, **"Wa Alaikum Assalam, Ahmed. How did you sleep?"** This reply means "And peace be upon you too." Ahmed replied, **"Alhamdulillah, I slept well." Alhamdulillah** means "Praise be to Allah," and it is used to express gratitude.

Ummi then asked Ahmed if he wanted to help water the plants. Ahmed's eyes lit up. "Yes, Ummi! I love helping with the plants!" he said. Together, they filled the watering cans. Ummi showed Ahmed how to gently pour the water so the plants could drink it up.

As they watered each plant, Ummi told Ahmed the names of the flowers. Ahmed listened carefully and repeated the names. "This one is a rose, and that one is a tulip," Ummi said. Ahmed nodded and smiled, "The garden looks so beautiful, Ummi."

After they finished watering the plants, Ahmed noticed some weeds in the garden. "Can I help pull out the weeds, Ummi?" he asked. Ummi nodded, "Of course, Ahmed. Thank you for your help." Together, they pulled out the weeds and made the garden look neat and tidy.

When they were done, Ahmed said, **"Shukran, Ummi, for teaching me about the plants." Shukran** means "Thank you." Ummi replied, **"Afwan, Ahmed. You did a great job helping today." Afwan** means "You're welcome."

Ahmed then ran to find his Abu, who was fixing a bike in the backyard. **"Assalamu Alaikum, Abu!"** Ahmed said. His Abu looked up and smiled, **"Wa Alaikum Assalam, Ahmed. Would you like to help me?"** Ahmed eagerly nodded and said, "Yes, Baba!" Together, they worked on the bike and soon it was fixed. **"Alhamdulillah,"** said Abu. **"Alhamdulillah,"** echoed Ahmed.

Later, Ahmed decided to visit his Jaddi and Jaddati. He loved spending time with them. As he entered their house, he called out, **"Assalamu Alaikum, Jaddi and Jaddati!"** His Jaddi responded, **"Wa Alaikum**

Assalam, Ahmed. It's good to see you!" Jaddati smiled warmly, "Come, Ahmed. I made your favorite cookies."

"Shukran, Jaddati," Ahmed said as he took a cookie. Jaddati replied, **"Afwan, dear. Enjoy!"** Ahmed felt happy and loved. He loved saying these special words because they made everyone feel good.

After a fun day with his grandparents, Ahmed went back home. On his way, he saw his friend, Ali. **"Assalamu Alaikum, Ali!"** Ahmed greeted him. **"Wa Alaikum Assalam, Ahmed!"** replied Ali. They played together until it was time to go home. Ahmed waved and said, **"Ma'assalama, Ali!"** Ma'assalama means "Goodbye" or "Go with safety." Ali waved back, **"Ma'assalama, Ahmed!"**

When Ahmed reached home, his little sister, Aisha, was waiting for him. **"Assalamu Alaikum, Aisha!"** Ahmed said gently. **"Wa Alaikum Assalam, Khuya!"** giggled Aisha. Ahmed hugged her and took her to their Ummi.

That night, as Ahmed got ready for bed, he thanked Allah for the wonderful day. **"Alhamdulillah for my family and friends,"** he whispered. Ummi came to tuck him in and kissed him on the forehead. **"Bismillah, sleep well, my dear Ahmed,"** she said. **Bismillah** means "In the name of Allah," and it is often said before starting something.

"Wa Alaikum Assalam, Ummi," Ahmed replied with a smile as he drifted off to sleep.

Every day, Ahmed used these special greetings and words: **"Assalamu Alaikum"** to say hello, **"Wa Alaikum Assalam"** to reply, **"Bismillah"** before starting something, **"Alhamdulillah"** to give thanks, **"Shukran"** to say thank you, **"Afwan"** to say you're welcome, and **"Ma'assalama"** to say goodbye.

Ahmed learned that these words were not just words; they were gifts that made everyone happy and brought peace. He loved sharing these gifts every day.

Moral of the Story: Always use kind words to make people happy and show respect.

Chapter 38

Understanding Qibla: The Direction of Prayer

Ahmed was a curious and happy little boy who loved learning new things. He lived with his Ummi, Abu, and his baby sister, Ikht Aisha. Every day, Ahmed would ask many questions about the world around him.

One day, after breakfast, Ahmed asked his Abu, "Baba, why do we always face a certain direction when we pray?" Abu smiled and said, "That's a very good question, Ahmed. We face the Qibla when we pray. The Qibla is the direction of the Kaaba in Mecca."

Ahmed's eyes grew wide with curiosity. "What is the Kaaba, Baba?" he asked. Abu explained, "The Kaaba is a very special building in Mecca, Saudi Arabia. It is the house of Allah, and all Muslims around the world face the Kaaba when they pray."

Abu decided to show Ahmed a picture of the Kaaba. "Look, Ahmed," he said, pointing to the picture. "This is the Kaaba. It is covered with a black cloth with beautiful golden designs. Muslims from all over the world come to visit the Kaaba during Hajj."

"Wow, Baba! It looks so beautiful!" Ahmed exclaimed. "But how do we know which way to face when we are far from the Kaaba?"

Abu explained, "In our home, we have a special tool called a compass that helps us find the Qibla. In mosques, there is a special place called the Mihrab. The Mihrab is a niche in the wall that shows everyone the direction of the Qibla. This way, we all face the right direction when we pray."

Ahmed was fascinated. He wanted to learn more. That afternoon, he and his Abu went to the mosque. As they entered, Ahmed saw the Mihrab. It was beautifully decorated and pointed towards the Qibla. "Assalamu Alaikum, Ahmed," greeted the imam. "Wa Alaikum Assalam," replied Ahmed.

The imam explained, "The Mihrab shows us the way to face the Kaaba. When we pray together, we all face the same direction, towards the Kaaba, showing that we are united."

Ahmed felt happy to learn about the Qibla. He thought it was amazing that all Muslims, no matter where they are in the world, face the same direction when they pray. He asked his Abu, "Baba, can we pray now?"

Abu smiled and said, "Of course, Ahmed. Let's say, 'Bismillah,' and start our prayer." They stood side by side, facing the Mihrab, and began their prayer.

When they finished, Ahmed felt a sense of peace. "Alhamdulillah," he said, thanking Allah for the wonderful lesson he learned today.

That night, as Ahmed got ready for bed, he thanked his Ummi and Abu for teaching him about the Qibla. "Shukran, Ummi. Shukran, Abu," he said. "Afwan, Ahmed," replied his Ummi. "We are glad you enjoyed learning about the Qibla."

As Ahmed lay in bed, he thought about how special it was to face the Kaaba when praying. He felt connected to Muslims all around the world. He drifted off to sleep with a smile, thinking about his next prayer.

Moral of the Story: Learning about our faith helps us feel closer to Allah and connected to others.

Chapter 39

The Role of Angels in Islam

Ahmed was a bright and curious little boy who loved to learn new things. He lived with his Ummi, Abu, and his baby sister, Ikht Aisha. Every night, before going to bed, Ahmed's Ummi would tell him stories about their faith.

One evening, after dinner, Ahmed asked his Ummi, "Ummi, can you tell me about angels? I heard they are very special in Islam." Ummi smiled and said, "Of course, Ahmed. Angels are indeed very special."

"Angels are created by Allah from light," Ummi began. "They are different from us because they do not eat or sleep, and they always obey Allah's commands. They help Allah with many important tasks."

Ahmed listened carefully as his Ummi continued. "One of the most important angels is Angel Jibril. He is known as the messenger angel. Angel Jibril brought Allah's messages to the prophets. He came to Prophet Muhammad (peace be upon him) and gave him the words of the Quran."

"Wow, Ummi! That's amazing!" Ahmed exclaimed. "What other angels are there?"

Ummi said, "There are many angels, Ahmed. For example, Angel Mika'il is in charge of providing rain and sustenance to all of Allah's creations. Angel Israfil will blow the trumpet on the Day of Judgment. And there are also angels who record our good and bad deeds."

"Record our deeds?" Ahmed asked, looking curious. "Yes," Ummi replied. "We have two angels with us all the time. They are called Kiraman Katibin. One angel sits on our right shoulder and writes down our good deeds, while the other angel sits on our left shoulder and writes down our bad deeds."

Ahmed looked at his shoulders and smiled. "I want my good deeds book to be very big!" he said. Ummi laughed gently, "That's a wonderful goal, Ahmed. Always try to do good things like helping others, saying kind words, and praying to Allah."

As they continued talking, Abu came into the room. "Assalamu Alaikum," he greeted them. "Wa Alaikum Assalam," Ahmed and Ummi replied.

"Ahmed is learning about angels," Ummi told Abu. "Oh, that's wonderful," Abu said. "Did you know that angels also protect us? They keep us safe and help us in many ways that we don't even see."

Ahmed's eyes grew wide with wonder. "SubhanAllah, that's so special!" he said. "Alhamdulillah for the angels."

"That's right, Ahmed," Abu said. "And when we pray, angels come close to us and listen to our prayers. They love it when we remember Allah."

Feeling grateful, Ahmed said, "Bismillah," and got ready for his bedtime prayer. He stood with his Abu and prayed, feeling happy knowing that angels were around him.

After the prayer, Ahmed said, "Shukran, Abu and Ummi, for teaching me about angels." "Afwan, Ahmed," replied his Abu. "We are glad you enjoyed learning about them."

As Ahmed lay in bed, he thought about all the angels and their important jobs. He felt safe and loved, knowing that Allah had created angels to help and protect everyone. He whispered, "Alhamdulillah for the angels," before drifting off to sleep.

Moral of the Story: Always remember that angels are around us, helping and protecting us, and they love when we do good deeds.

Chapter 40

The Concept of Shura: Consultation

Ahmed was a bright and cheerful little boy who loved spending time with his family. He lived with his Ummi, Abu, and his baby sister, Ikht Aisha. Every day, he learned new things from his parents and enjoyed sharing stories with them.

One afternoon, Ahmed came home from school looking puzzled. His Ummi noticed and asked, "Assalamu Alaikum, Ahmed. What's on your mind?" Ahmed replied, "Wa Alaikum Assalam, Ummi. Today, our teacher talked about making decisions, and I didn't understand it very well."

Ummi smiled and said, "Let's talk about it together. In Islam, we have a special way of making decisions called Shura. Shura means consultation, and it helps us make good choices by asking others for their advice and opinions."

Ahmed was curious and asked, "How does Shura work, Ummi?" Ummi explained, "Shura means we ask our family and friends for their thoughts before making a decision. This way, we get different ideas and can choose the best option." Just then, Abu came into the room. "Assalamu Alaikum," he greeted them. "Wa Alaikum Assalam," Ahmed and Ummi replied. Ummi told Abu about their discussion. Abu nodded and said, "Ahmed, let's show you how Shura works with a real example."

Abu said, "Let's decide what to do this weekend. We can use Shura to make our choice. Ahmed, you can ask everyone in the family what they would like to do."

Ahmed was excited. He went to his baby sister, Aisha, and said, "Assalamu Alaikum, Aisha! What would you like to do this weekend?" Aisha giggled and said, "Play in the park!" Next, Ahmed asked his Ummi, "Ummi, what would you like to do this weekend?" Ummi thought for a moment and said, "I would love to visit Jaddi and Jaddati." Then, Ahmed asked his Abu, "Abu, what about you?" Abu smiled and said, "I think we should go to the library and read some books."

Finally, Ahmed shared his own idea. "I want to have a picnic by the lake," he said. Abu said, "Great job, Ahmed. Now, let's sit together and discuss all these ideas."

They all sat down and started their Shura. Ummi said, "I like the idea of a picnic. We can enjoy the outdoors and bring some of our favorite foods." Abu added, "And we can also visit the library on the way back home."

Ahmed was happy and said, "And maybe we can go to the park near the lake so Aisha can play too!" Everyone agreed that this was a wonderful plan.

"Bismillah," said Abu, "Let's plan our picnic day!" They made a list of what to bring and who would do each task. Ahmed was in charge of packing the snacks, Ummi would prepare the sandwiches, Abu would bring the picnic blanket, and Aisha would bring her favorite toy.

That weekend, the family had a fantastic day. They visited the library, enjoyed a picnic by the lake, and played in the park. Ahmed felt very happy and proud that they made the decision together using Shura.

That night, as Ahmed got ready for bed, he thanked his Ummi and Abu for teaching him about Shura. "Shukran, Ummi. Shukran, Abu," he said. "Afwan, Ahmed," replied his Ummi. "We are glad you enjoyed learning about Shura." As Ahmed lay in bed, he thought about how special it was to make decisions together. He whispered, "Alhamdulillah for Shura," before drifting off to sleep.

Moral of the Story: Working together and asking for advice helps us make the best decisions.

Chapter 41

The Importance of Knowledge in Islam

Ahmed was a bright and curious little boy who loved to ask questions. He lived with his Ummi, Abu, and his baby sister, Ikht Aisha. Every day, he went to school and learned new things. Ahmed loved reading books and discovering the world around him.

One evening, after dinner, Ahmed asked his Abu, "Baba, why is learning so important in Islam?" Abu smiled and said, "That's a great question, Ahmed. In Islam, seeking knowledge is very important because it helps us understand the world and become better people."

Ummi joined them and said, "Ahmed, let me tell you something special. The first word revealed in the Quran was 'Iqra,' which means 'Read.' This shows us how much Allah wants us to learn and seek knowledge."

Ahmed was fascinated. "Wow, Ummi! I didn't know that. What else does the Quran say about knowledge?" he asked. Abu explained, "The Quran encourages us to learn about everything, from science and math to understanding right and wrong. The more we know, the better we can help others and worship Allah."

The next day, Ahmed was excited to go to school. He told his friends, "Did you know that learning is very important in Islam? The Quran tells us to read and seek knowledge!" His friends listened eagerly as Ahmed shared what he learned from his Abu and Ummi.

At home, Ahmed loved reading books with his Jaddi and Jaddati. One afternoon, Jaddi showed Ahmed a special book. "This is a book of Hadith, Ahmed. It contains the sayings of Prophet Muhammad (peace be upon him). The Prophet said that seeking knowledge is an obligation for every Muslim."

"Assalamu Alaikum, Jaddi," Ahmed greeted him as he sat down. "Wa Alaikum Assalam, Ahmed," Jaddi replied. "Let me read you a Hadith. The Prophet said, 'Seeking knowledge is a duty upon every Muslim.' This means we should always try to learn new things."

Ahmed listened carefully. "Shukran, Jaddi, for teaching me this," he said. "Afwan, Ahmed," Jaddi replied. "Remember, knowledge helps us grow and become better Muslims."

One day, Ahmed's school organized a science fair. Ahmed decided to participate with a project about plants. He spent days reading and learning about how plants grow. He even asked his Ummi and Abu for help. "Bismillah," he would say each time he started his work.

The day of the science fair arrived, and Ahmed was very excited. He explained his project to everyone, sharing the knowledge he had gained. At the end of the fair, Ahmed's project won a prize! "Alhamdulillah!" he exclaimed with joy. "I am so happy I learned so much about plants!"

His Abu and Ummi were very proud. "Ahmed, you worked very hard and used your knowledge well. We are proud of you," said Abu. "Shukran, Baba," Ahmed replied.

That night, as Ahmed got ready for bed, he thanked his Ummi and Abu for encouraging him to seek knowledge. "Shukran, Ummi. Shukran, Abu," he said. "Afwan, Ahmed," they replied. "Remember, the more you learn, the more you can help others and please Allah."

As Ahmed lay in bed, he thought about how special it was to learn new things. He whispered, "Alhamdulillah for knowledge," before drifting off to sleep.

Moral of the Story: Seeking knowledge helps us grow, understand the world, and become better person.

Chapter 42

The Story of the Islamic Dress Code

Ahmed was a bright and curious little boy who loved to learn about his faith. He lived with his Ummi, Abu, and his baby sister, Ikht Aisha. Every day, he had many questions about Islam.

One day, after school, Ahmed asked his Ummi, "Ummi, why do we wear certain clothes in Islam?" Ummi smiled and said, "That's a great question, Ahmed. In Islam, we have a dress code that helps us stay modest and respectful."

Ummi explained, "For both men and women, dressing modestly means covering our bodies properly and wearing loose-fitting clothes. It shows respect for ourselves and others. It's also a way to show that we love and follow Allah's guidance."

Ahmed was curious about the different types of clothes. "Ummi, can you tell me more about the clothes we wear?" he asked.

Ummi nodded and said, "For men, it's important to wear clothes that cover from the navel to the knees. Many men wear a long shirt called a thobe, which covers the whole body. It is comfortable and modest. They can also wear pants and shirts, as long as they are not too tight."

Ahmed listened carefully. "And what about women, Ummi?" he asked.

Ummi continued, "For women, it is important to cover everything except the face and hands. Women wear a hijab to cover their hair. They also wear long dresses or skirts and loose-fitting tops. Some women also wear an abaya, which is a long, black cloak that covers the whole body."

Ahmed wanted to see these clothes in real life, so Ummi suggested, "Let's look at some pictures together, Ahmed." They went to the living room and found a book with pictures of people wearing traditional Islamic clothing. Ahmed pointed to the pictures and said, "These clothes look so nice and respectful!"

Later, Ahmed and his family went to the market. At the market, Ahmed saw many people wearing different types of modest clothing. He saw men wearing thobes and women wearing hijabs and abayas. "Look, Ummi! Everyone looks so respectful and beautiful," Ahmed said with a smile.

Ali's Ummi smiled and said, "We wear these clothes to show our respect for Allah's teachings and to stay modest." Ahmed felt happy and proud to be part of a community that valued modesty.

That evening, the family went to visit Jaddi and Jaddati. When they arrived, Ahmed greeted them, "Assalamu Alaikum, Jaddi and Jaddati!"

His Jaddi replied, "Wa Alaikum Assalam, Ahmed. It's good to see you!" Ahmed was excited to share what he had learned. "Jaddi, Jaddati, I learned about the Islamic dress code. It's about being modest and respectful," he said proudly.

Jaddati smiled warmly and said, "That's wonderful, Ahmed. Dressing modestly is an important part of our faith. It shows that we follow Allah's guidance and respect ourselves and others." During their visit, Ahmed noticed that his Jaddi wore a thobe, and his Jaddati wore a hijab and an abaya. He felt proud to be part of a family that followed the teachings of Islam.

That night, as Ahmed got ready for bed, he thanked his Ummi and Abu for teaching him about the Islamic dress code. "Shukran, Ummi. Shukran, Abu," he said. "Afwan, Ahmed," they replied. "We are glad you enjoyed learning about it."

As Ahmed lay in bed, he thought about how important it was to dress modestly and follow Allah's guidance. He whispered, "Alhamdulillah for the beautiful teachings of Islam," before drifting off to sleep.

Moral of the Story: Dressing modestly shows respect for ourselves and others, and helps us follow Allah's guidance.

Chapter 43

Understanding Qadr: Divine Destiny

Ahmed was a bright and curious little boy who loved exploring the world around him. He lived with his Ummi, Abu, and his baby sister, Ikht Aisha. Every day, he was eager to learn new things and often asked many questions about life and faith.

One evening, Ahmed's family gathered in the living room after dinner. "Baba," Ahmed asked, "what does Qadr mean?" Abu smiled and said, "That's a great question, Ahmed. Qadr means divine destiny. It is the belief that Allah has a plan for everything and that everything happens for a reason."

Ummi joined in and said, "Qadr teaches us to trust in Allah's plan, even when we don't understand why things happen the way they do. It reminds us that Allah knows best."

Ahmed was curious. "Can you tell me more about how Qadr works, Ummi?" he asked. Ummi nodded and said, "Let's think about a tree. A tree starts as a tiny seed. With water, sunlight, and time, it grows into a big tree. Allah knows how tall the tree will grow and when it will bloom. This is like Qadr. Allah knows everything that will happen in our lives."

Just then, Abu said, "Ahmed, let me share a story to help you understand better." He began, "There was a man who planned to go on a journey. He prepared everything and set out early in the morning.

But on his way, his cart broke down. The man was very sad and thought his journey was ruined."

Ahmed listened carefully. Abu continued, "While the man was fixing his cart, a friend came by and helped him. Together, they fixed the cart and the man continued his journey. Later, he found out that there was a big storm ahead. Because his cart broke down, he missed the storm and stayed safe. The man realized that Allah's plan was better than his own."

"SubhanAllah, Baba! That's amazing!" Ahmed exclaimed. "So, even when things don't go as we plan, it might be part of Allah's plan to protect us?"

"Exactly, Ahmed," said Abu. "We must trust that Allah always has a good reason for everything that happens."

The next day, Ahmed went to school and shared what he learned with his friends. "Did you know that Qadr means divine destiny? It teaches us to trust in Allah's plan," he told them. His friends were fascinated and asked Ahmed to explain more.

At home, Ahmed decided to help his Ummi in the kitchen. "Bismillah," he said as he started. While helping, he accidentally spilled some flour. "Oh no, Ummi! I made a mess!" he exclaimed.

Ummi smiled and said, "It's okay, Ahmed. Let's clean it up together. Sometimes, mistakes happen, but we can learn from them and trust that everything will be alright."

That night, as Ahmed got ready for bed, he thought about all he had learned. He whispered, "Alhamdulillah for teaching me about Qadr and trusting Allah's plan."

Just before he fell asleep, his Abu came to his room. "Ahmed, remember that Allah loves us and wants the best for us. Always trust in His plan," he said gently. Ahmed nodded and said, "Shukran, Baba. I will always remember that."

As Ahmed lay in bed, he felt peaceful knowing that Allah was taking care of everything. He whispered, "Alhamdulillah for Allah's plan," before drifting off to sleep.

Moral of the Story: Trust in Allah's plan, even when things don't go as expected, because Allah knows what is best for us.

Chapter 44

The Story of Halaal Food

Ahmed was a bright and curious little boy who loved exploring the world around him. He lived with his Ummi, Abu, and his baby sister, Ikht Aisha. Every day, he learned new things and enjoyed asking questions about everything he saw.

One day, after school, Ahmed came home feeling hungry. He went to the kitchen and saw his Ummi preparing dinner. "Assalamu Alaikum, Ummi!" he greeted her. "Wa Alaikum Assalam, Ahmed," she replied with a smile. Ahmed asked, "Ummi, what are we having for dinner?"

Ummi replied, "We are having chicken, rice, and vegetables." Ahmed watched as his Ummi cooked. He noticed that she was very careful with the ingredients she used. "Ummi, why do you always check everything before cooking?" he asked.

Ummi explained, "Ahmed, in Islam, we eat halaal food. Halaal means the food is allowed for us to eat according to our religion. We have to make sure everything is clean and prepared the right way."

Ahmed was curious. "What makes food halaal, Ummi?" he asked. Ummi smiled and said, "For meat to be halaal, it must come from an animal that is healthy and treated kindly. When the animal is prepared for us to eat, we say 'Bismillah' and 'Allahu Akbar' to thank Allah for the food."

Just then, Abu walked into the kitchen. "Assalamu Alaikum," he greeted them. "Wa Alaikum Assalam," Ahmed and Ummi replied. Ahmed told his Abu about their discussion.

Abu said, "Ahmed, let's go to the grocery store and find some halaal food together." Ahmed was excited and said, "Yes, Baba! Let's go!"

At the grocery store, they looked for a halaal section. Ahmed saw a sign that said "Halaal" and pointed it out to his Abu. "Look, Baba, there's the halaal section!" he exclaimed. Abu smiled and said, "Great job, Ahmed! Let's see what they have."

They picked out some halaal meat, rice, and vegetables. Ahmed noticed a special label on the packages. "Baba, what does this label mean?" he asked. Abu explained, "This label shows that the food is halaal. It means the food follows all the rules and is safe for us to eat."

When they got home, Ummi was waiting for them. "Did you find some good halaal food?" she asked. "Yes, Ummi!" Ahmed replied. "We found halaal meat and checked the labels on the packages."

That evening, Ummi prepared a delicious dinner with the halaal food they bought. They all sat down together and said, "Bismillah," before starting their meal. Ahmed felt happy and grateful.

Later that night, as Ahmed was brushing his teeth, he thought about the importance of eating halaal food. He realized that by following these rules, he was not only staying healthy but also showing his love for Allah. Ahmed felt proud and happy.

Before going to bed, Ahmed hugged his Ummi and Abu. "Shukran, Ummi. Shukran, Abu, for teaching me about halaal food," he said. "Afwan, Ahmed," they replied. "We are glad you enjoyed learning about it." As Ahmed snuggled under his blanket, with a big smile on his face, he closed his eyes and whispered, "Alhamdulillah for halaal food and for my family." Then he drifted off to sleep, feeling loved and blessed.

Moral of the Story: Eating halaal food helps us stay healthy and follow Allah's guidance.

Chapter 45

The Importance of Fasting Beyond Ramadan

One day, Ahmed came home from school feeling thoughtful. He went to the kitchen and saw his Ummi preparing dinner. "Assalamu Alaikum, Ummi!" he greeted her. "Wa Alaikum Assalam, Ahmed," she replied with a smile. Ahmed asked, "Ummi, I know we fast during Ramadan, but are there other times we can fast too?"

Ummi smiled and said, "That's a great question, Ahmed. Yes, there are other times when Muslims can fast. Fasting helps us become closer to Allah, and it also teaches us patience and self-control."

Ahmed was curious to learn more. "When else can we fast, Ummi?" he asked. Ummi explained, "There are special days throughout the year when we can fast. For example, fasting on Mondays and Thursdays is a good practice. The Prophet Muhammad (peace be upon him) used to fast on these days."

Just then, Abu walked into the kitchen. "Assalamu Alaikum," he greeted them. "Wa Alaikum Assalam," Ahmed and Ummi replied. Ahmed told his Abu about their discussion.

Abu said, "Ahmed, fasting outside of Ramadan has many benefits. It helps us remember Allah and keeps us mindful of our actions. Fasting on the Day of Arafah, for example, is very special. It is a day when Allah forgives our sins."

Ahmed listened carefully. "Baba, what other special days are there for fasting?" he asked. Abu continued, "There is also Ashura, the 10th day of Muharram. Fasting on this day is a way to seek forgiveness from Allah and remember important events in Islamic history."

Ummi added, "We can also fast six days in the month of Shawwal, right after Ramadan. This is called the fast of Shawwal, and it is like fasting for the whole year if we complete these six days along with Ramadan."

Ahmed nodded, understanding the importance. "SubhanAllah, fasting is really special!" he said. "Yes, Ahmed," Abu agreed. "It is a way to show our love for Allah and to become better people."

One day, Ahmed decided he wanted to try fasting on a Monday. He woke up early and said, "Bismillah," before starting his fast. Throughout the day, he felt hungry but remembered why he was fasting. He prayed and asked Allah for strength.

That evening, as the sun set, Ahmed sat down with his family to break his fast. "Alhamdulillah," he said, feeling grateful. Ummi and Abu were proud of him. "You did a wonderful job, Ahmed," said Ummi. "Fasting helps us appreciate the food we have and reminds us to be thankful."

After dinner, Ahmed and his family went for a walk in the park. As they walked, Ahmed felt a sense of peace and joy. He realized how fasting brought him closer to his family and to Allah.

As they reached home, the sky was filled with stars. Ahmed looked up and said, "Alhamdulillah for this beautiful night and for all the blessings." He felt grateful and content.

Later, as Ahmed was getting ready for bed, he remembered the lessons of the day. He hugged his Ummi and Abu tightly and said, "Shukran for teaching me about fasting, and for a wonderful day." "Afwan, Ahmed," they replied. "We are proud of you for learning and practicing your faith."

With a heart full of gratitude and happiness, Ahmed lay down to sleep. He knew that fasting was an important part of his faith, and he was excited to continue learning and growing. He whispered a quiet prayer of thanks before closing his eyes, feeling peaceful and loved.

Moral of the Story: Fasting helps us become closer to Allah, teaches us patience, and reminds us to be thankful for what we have.

Chapter 46

The Concept of Amanah: Trustworthiness

Ahmed was a bright and curious little boy who loved learning about his faith. He lived with his Ummi, Abu, and his baby sister, Ikht Aisha.

One afternoon, Ahmed's teacher at school announced that there would be a special treasure hunt the next day. All the students were excited. "Each of you will get a map," the teacher said. "Follow the map, and you will find a treasure. Remember to take good care of your map."

Ahmed couldn't wait to tell his family. When he got home, he ran to the kitchen. "Assalamu Alaikum, Ummi!" he greeted her. "Wa Alaikum Assalam, Ahmed!" she replied. Ahmed excitedly told his Ummi about the treasure hunt. "Ummi, I have to take care of my map and not lose it," he said.

Ummi smiled and said, "Ahmed, that is very important. Taking care of the map is your Amanah. It means being trustworthy and responsible."

The next day at school, the teacher gave each student a map. Ahmed held his map carefully. "Bismillah," he said before starting his treasure hunt. He followed the map's directions, making sure he didn't lose it.

As Ahmed walked, he saw his friend Sara looking sad. "What's wrong, Sara?" he asked. "I lost my map," she said, almost in tears. Ahmed remembered what his Ummi had said about Amanah. He thought for a moment and then had an idea.

"Sara, you can share my map," Ahmed offered. Sara's face lit up. "Shukran, Ahmed!" she said. "Afwan, Sara," Ahmed replied with a smile.

Together, they followed the map's directions and found the treasure – a box of colorful stickers. They were so happy. "We did it!" Ahmed exclaimed. "Yes, we did! Shukran for helping me, Ahmed," Sara said.

When Ahmed got home, he couldn't wait to tell his family about the treasure hunt. "Assalamu Alaikum, Ummi and Abu!" he greeted them. "Wa Alaikum Assalam, Ahmed," they replied. Ahmed shared his story about taking care of the map and helping Sara.

Abu said, "MashaAllah, Ahmed. You showed great Amanah today. You were trustworthy by taking care of your map and responsible by helping your friend."

That evening, after dinner, Ahmed's family sat together in the living room. They decided to read a story from the Quran about the Prophet

Muhammad (peace be upon him). "Did you know," Abu said, "that the Prophet Muhammad was known as Al-Amin, which means 'the trustworthy one'? People trusted him because he was always honest and responsible."

Ahmed felt proud to be following the example of the Prophet. Before heading to bed, he hugged his Ummi and Abu. "Shukran for teaching me about Amanah and for the lovely story," he said. "Afwan, Ahmed. We are proud of you," they replied.

As Ahmed lay in bed, he thought about his day. He felt happy knowing he had kept his Amanah by taking care of the map and helping Sara. He whispered a quiet prayer, "Alhamdulillah for teaching me about trustworthiness and for my loving family."

With a heart full of gratitude, Ahmed closed his eyes and drifted off to sleep, dreaming of more ways he could practice Amanah in his everyday life.

Moral of the Story: Being trustworthy means keeping promises, taking care of responsibilities, and helping others.

Chapter 47

Understanding Qiyam: Standing in Prayer

One evening, after dinner, Ahmed noticed his Abu getting ready for prayer. "Assalamu Alaikum, Baba," Ahmed said. "Wa Alaikum Assalam, Ahmed," replied Abu. "What are you doing, Baba?" Ahmed asked.

Abu smiled and said, "I am getting ready for Qiyam, Ahmed. Qiyam means standing in prayer, especially during Tahajjud, the night prayer."

Ahmed was curious. "What is Tahajjud, Baba?" he asked. Abu explained, "Tahajjud is a special prayer we perform in the night, after Isha prayer and before Fajr prayer. It is a time when we can talk to Allah and ask for His help and guidance."

Ahmed thought for a moment and said, "Can I join you, Baba?" Abu nodded and said, "Of course, Ahmed. But first, let's talk to your Ummi."

They went to the kitchen where Ummi was cleaning up. "Assalamu Alaikum, Ummi," Ahmed greeted her. "Wa Alaikum Assalam, Ahmed and Abu," she replied. Ahmed told her about his plan to join Abu for Tahajjud. Ummi smiled and said, "That's a wonderful idea, Ahmed. Remember to say 'Bismillah' before you start."

That night, Ahmed set his alarm clock to wake up before Fajr. When the alarm rang, he quietly got up and went to his Abu's room. "Bismillah," he whispered as he joined Abu in the living room.

They stood together and began their prayer. Ahmed felt a sense of peace as he stood in Qiyam. Abu recited beautiful verses from the Quran, and Ahmed listened carefully. After they finished praying, Abu made a special dua, asking Allah for blessings and guidance.

"Alhamdulillah," said Ahmed, feeling happy. "That was very special, Baba. I feel closer to Allah."

The next morning, at breakfast, Ahmed excitedly told his Ummi about the Tahajjud prayer. "Ummi, it was so peaceful. I loved standing in Qiyam and listening to Baba recite the Quran," he said.

Ummi hugged Ahmed and said, "MashaAllah, Ahmed. Qiyam during Tahajjud is a special time to connect with Allah. It teaches us patience and helps us grow stronger in our faith."

Later that day, Ahmed and his family visited Jaddi and Jaddati. Ahmed was excited to share what he had learned. "Jaddi, Jaddati, I prayed Tahajjud with Baba last night. It was so peaceful, and I felt very close to Allah," he said proudly. Jaddati smiled warmly and said, "That's wonderful, Ahmed. Tahajjud and standing in Qiyam are beautiful ways to connect with Allah and ask for His guidance."

That evening, as the sun began to set, Ahmed and his family gathered for Maghrib prayer. After the prayer, they sat together and talked about the importance of prayer in their lives. Abu said, "Ahmed, you did a great job with Tahajjud. Remember that standing in Qiyam helps us stay strong in our faith and seek Allah's blessings."

Ahmed nodded, feeling proud and happy. Before heading to bed, he hugged his Ummi and Abu tightly. "Shukran for teaching me about Qiyam and Tahajjud," he said. "Afwan, Ahmed. We are proud of you," they replied.

As Ahmed lay in bed, he thought about the peaceful night prayer and how it made him feel closer to Allah. He whispered a quiet prayer, "Alhamdulillah for Tahajjud and for my loving family."

With a heart full of gratitude, Ahmed closed his eyes and drifted off to sleep, dreaming of more ways he could practice Qiyam in his everyday life.

Moral of the Story: Standing in prayer, especially during Tahajjud, helps us grow closer to Allah and strengthens our faith.

Chapter 48

The Story of the Quranic Recitation: Tajweed

One day, Ahmed saw his Abu reading the Quran with a melodious and precise voice. "Assalamu Alaikum, Baba," Ahmed said. "Wa Alaikum Assalam, Ahmed," replied Abu. Ahmed watched in awe and asked, "Baba, how do you recite the Quran so beautifully?"

Abu smiled and said, "I use Tajweed, Ahmed. Tajweed means reciting the Quran with the correct pronunciation and following specific rules. Would you like to learn?"

Ahmed's eyes lit up with excitement. "Yes, Baba! I want to learn Tajweed," he replied eagerly.

Abu said, "Alright, let's begin. Abu and Ahmed sat down with the Quran. "Ahmed, Tajweed helps us recite the Quran the way it was revealed to Prophet Muhammad (peace be upon him). It is important to pronounce the letters correctly and to use the right sounds," Abu explained.

"Let's start with the rule of Ikhfa," Abu continued. "Ikhfa means to hide. When we recite, sometimes we come across letters that we need to pronounce softly through our nose. This happens when a Noon Saakin or Tanween comes before certain letters."

Ahmed looked puzzled, so Abu explained further. "Noon Saakin is a letter 'noon' with a sukoon, which means it has no vowel sound. Tanween are the double vowels at the end of words that sound like 'an', 'in', or 'un'. When these appear before certain letters, we use Ikhfa to blend the sounds smoothly."

Abu demonstrated by reciting a few verses, and Ahmed repeated after him, trying to make the sounds correctly. "Good job, Ahmed! Now let's learn about Ghunna," Abu said. "Ghunna is a nasal sound that you hold for two counts, like a gentle hum in your nose." Ahmed practiced the Ghunna sound, enjoying the way it made his recitation flow smoothly.

As they continued practicing, Ahmed's recitation improved. "Alhamdulillah, Baba, this is really interesting," he said, feeling proud of his progress.

The next day, during Quran class at school, Ahmed raised his hand and asked the teacher if he could recite a verse using Tajweed. The teacher smiled and said, "Of course, Ahmed."

Ahmed recited a verse from the Quran, using the rules of Tajweed he had learned. The teacher and his classmates were impressed. "MashaAllah, Ahmed! That was beautiful," the teacher said. Ahmed felt proud and thanked Allah for helping him.

That evening, Ahmed's family gathered for Maghrib prayer. After the prayer, they talked about the importance of reciting the Quran correctly. Abu said, "Ahmed, you did a great job with Tajweed. Remember, reciting the Quran with Tajweed helps us respect the words of Allah and understand their meanings better."

Ahmed nodded, feeling proud and happy. Before heading to bed, he hugged his Ummi and Abu tightly. "Shukran for teaching me about Tajweed," he said. "Afwan, Ahmed. We are proud of you," they replied.

As Ahmed lay in bed, he thought about how important it was to recite the Quran correctly. He whispered a quiet prayer, "Alhamdulillah for Tajweed and for my loving family."

With a heart full of gratitude, Ahmed closed his eyes and drifted off to sleep, dreaming of more ways he could practice Tajweed in his everyday life.

Moral of the Story: Reciting the Quran with Tajweed helps us respect the words of Allah and understand their meanings better.

Chapter 49

The Role of the Quranic Schools: Madrasah

One morning, Ahmed woke up excited because it was his first day at the local madrasah. "Bismillah," Ahmed whispered to himself as he got dressed. He was eager to learn more about the Quran and his faith.

After breakfast, Ahmed and his Abu walked to the madrasah. "Assalamu Alaikum, Baba," Ahmed said. "Wa Alaikum Assalam, Ahmed," replied Abu.

When they arrived, they were greeted by the teacher, Ustadh Karim. "Assalamu Alaikum, Ahmed. Welcome to the madrasah," Ustadh Karim said warmly. "Wa Alaikum Assalam, Ustadh," Ahmed replied. Ahmed saw other children sitting in a circle, ready to learn.

"Today, we will start with a beautiful surah from the Quran," Ustadh Karim began. He recited the verses, and the children repeated after him. Ahmed listened carefully, trying to pronounce each word correctly. He felt proud as he echoed the beautiful words of the Quran.

During the break, Ahmed made new friends. He met a boy named Bilal. "Assalamu Alaikum, Ahmed," Bilal greeted him. "Wa Alaikum Assalam, Bilal," Ahmed replied. They talked about their favorite surahs and how excited they were to learn more. Bilal shared his experience at the madrasah and assured Ahmed that he would love it.

After the break, Ustadh Karim taught the class about the importance of the Quran. "The Quran is our guide," he explained. "It teaches us how to live a good life and be kind to others. It's important to recite it with understanding and love." Ahmed nodded, understanding the significance of his lessons.

Ustadh Karim also explained the history of the Quran and how it was revealed to the Prophet Muhammad (peace be upon him) over 1,400 years ago.

Ahmed learned about the different rules of Tajweed, which are the rules for reciting the Quran correctly. Ustadh Karim explained how Tajweed helps us pronounce the words properly, so we respect the words of Allah. Ahmed found it fascinating and was eager to practice more.

At the end of the day, Ahmed felt happy and proud. He couldn't wait to tell his family about his first day at madrasah. When he got home, he found his Ummi and Abu in the kitchen. "Assalamu Alaikum, Ummi! Assalamu Alaikum, Baba!" Ahmed greeted them.

"Wa Alaikum Assalam, Ahmed," they replied. Ahmed shared his experiences from the day. "I learned a new surah, made a friend named Bilal, and learned about Tajweed," he said excitedly. "That's wonderful, Ahmed," Ummi said. "Learning at madrasah will help you understand the Quran better and become a good Muslim. Remember, the Quran is our guide in life."

That night, as Ahmed was getting ready for bed, he felt grateful for his first day at madrasah. "Alhamdulillah for such a wonderful day," he whispered. He hugged his Ummi and Abu tightly. "Shukran for sending me to madrasah," he said. "Afwan, Ahmed. We are proud of you," they replied.

As Ahmed lay in bed, he thought about all the things he would learn at madrasah. He felt happy knowing that he was taking steps to become a better Muslim. He looked forward to reciting the Quran with Tajweed and understanding its meanings. With a heart full of gratitude, he closed his eyes and drifted off to sleep, excited for the next day.

Moral of the Story: Madrasahs help us learn about the Quran and grow in our faith, guiding us to live good and kind lives.

Chapter 50

Understanding the Concept of Barakah: Blessings

Ali loved spending time with his family. One sunny morning, his Abu said, "Ali, today we will learn about Barakah, which means blessings." Ali was curious and said, "Bismillah," ready to start his day.

Abu explained, "Ali, Barakah means having blessings from Allah in our lives. It can be in many forms, like good health, a loving family, or even the food we eat." Ali listened carefully, eager to learn more.

Later, Ali's Ummi joined them in the kitchen. She said, "Ali, do you see this bread? It is a blessing from Allah. We should always say, 'Alhamdulillah' to thank Allah for our food." She continued, "Every meal we eat is a gift, and we must never forget to show our gratitude." Ali repeated, "Alhamdulillah," and smiled at his Ummi, feeling thankful for the delicious food they had.

In the afternoon, Ali's Jaddi came to visit. He said, "Ali, do you know that playing with your friends is also a blessing?" Jaddi shared stories of his childhood, playing games and laughing with his friends. "Always be grateful for the joy and fun in your life," Jaddi said. Ali nodded, understanding that even his playtime was a blessing. He promised to always appreciate his friends and the fun times they shared together.

Ali's Akhi, Yusuf, then showed him a small plant growing in their garden. "Look, Ali, this plant is growing well because of Barakah. We take care of it, and Allah blesses it to grow," Yusuf explained. Ali helped water the plant and felt happy to be part of nurturing something. "Taking care of living things brings blessings," Yusuf added. Ali smiled, knowing that by caring for the plant, he was also bringing Barakah into his life.

In the evening, Ali's Ukhti, Fatima, came to read him a story. "Ali, spending time with family is one of the biggest blessings," she said. "When we are together, we should say, 'Alhamdulillah,' for having each other." She read him a story about a family that loved and supported each other, showing how family is a true blessing. Ali hugged his Ukhti and said, "Alhamdulillah for my family." He felt warm and loved, realizing how special his family was.

Before bed, Ali's Baba talked to him about kindness. "Ali, being kind to others brings Barakah into our lives. When we help others, Allah blesses us even more," Baba explained. He shared examples of small acts of kindness, like sharing toys or helping someone in need. Ali thought about how he could be kind to his friends and family. He decided to be more helpful and considerate, knowing it would bring blessings.

Ali's Jaddati then joined them and shared a special moment. She said, "Ali, do you remember how we help the needy? That is a way to bring Barakah into our lives. When we give to others, Allah gives us more blessings." She told him stories of how their family had helped others, and how those acts of kindness had brought joy and blessings back to them. Ali remembered donating clothes and toys to those in need and felt proud. He promised to continue being generous and caring.

As Ali lay in bed, he thought about all the blessings he had learned about. He realized that Barakah was everywhere in his life, from the food he ate to the love of his family. He whispered, "Alhamdulillah," thanking Allah for all the blessings. Ali understood that Barakah wasn't just about big things, but also the small, everyday moments that made life beautiful. He felt happy and peaceful, knowing that Allah's blessings were always with him.

Moral of the Story: Always be thankful for the blessings in your life, both big and small.

www.ingramcontent.com/pod-product-compliance
Lightning Source LLC
Chambersburg PA
CBHW051157290426
44109CB00022B/2491